the Pastor's Wife:
balancing her multiple relationships

by Pamela Hoover Heim

Published by Harvest Publications
©2001 by Pamela Hoover Heim
Cover and text design by Sharon Nelsen

ISBN: 0-935797-48-3

Unless otherwise noted, all Scriptures are taken from The Holy Bible: New International Version. *Copyright 1978 by the International Bible Society. Used by permission of Zondervan Bible Publishers.*

All rights reserved. No part of this book may be reproduced in any manner whatsoever without written permission from the publisher, except in the case of brief quotations embodied in critical articles and reviews.

Women's Ministries
Global Church Enrichment
Baptist General Conference
2002 S. Arlington Heights Rd.
Arlington Heights, IL 60005-4193
800-323-4215 • www.bgcworld.org

Introduction

Pastors' wives* weren't on my job description when I began ministry as a denominational leader about ten years ago. Traveling around the country as director of women's ministries, I met pastors' wives, talked with them, and gave them counsel when they sought it. Some called me to talk about problems they faced. Job description or not, I cared about ministry wives and was committed to serving them.

I began a quarterly newsletter for pastors' wives in the denomination I served. The response was overwhelmingly positive. Some told me they went to the mailbox hoping the next issue was there. Some said the topic I addressed invariably hit the mark of the current problem they were facing. Some of their husbands confessed that they read the newsletter, found it helpful, and used its content in a variety of ways. I knew I had touched a felt need.

This book is a compilation of the articles I wrote for those newsletters. It's not a comprehensive or definitive book on the role of the pastor's wife. It simply deals with some real issues faced by real women living with real husbands who pastor real churches. As I began reworking newsletter articles into book chapters, it seemed to me I was dealing with the variety of relationships in which a pastor's wife finds herself: relating to God, to herself, to her family, to her church, and to people in general.

I know some pastors' wives will read this book and privately work through the section "For Personal Meditation and Group Discussion" in each chapter. I believe they'll find this personal study helpful.

I suggest, however, that pastors' wives gain maximum impact by using this book in a pastors' wives small group. Each chapter is short enough to read at the group's gathering (so no prior preparation is needed).

If you're not already a part of a pastors' wives support group, I encourage you to form one. In a multi-staff church, a group could be made up of ministry wives from your church. Or you may feel you want to gather with pastors' wives from your own denomination who live in your vicinity. If these types of groups work for you, great! If you'd rather, gather a group composed of women from a variety of denominations. My observation is that sometimes there's more open sharing in those groups where members don't meet or work together in other settings.

Whatever grouping you form, take the initiative to make the phone calls and take other steps to gather your peers to explore the idea of beginning a group. Your first meeting might be a brunch, lunch, or dessert. In this initial meeting, discuss how often and where to meet. Deal with such issues as whether or not you want food or refreshments at your meetings. Think through the details.

However you get a group together and whatever physical details you decide, you must have some guidelines for the group. Keep them few and simple. The goal is to nurture a safe place for women to explore, learn, and grow. I recommend at least these guidelines:

- Confidentiality is a must. All sharing done in the group stays in the group. This means not sharing group discus-

sions with anybody outside the group, even a husband. Never talk outside the group with another group member about a group member who isn't present; this is gossiping.
- No group member should be pressured to reveal more than she cares to. Gentle questioning for clarity? Yes. Aggressive probing for details? No.
- The group is not a counseling session. Nobody gives advice unless it's asked for. Nobody monopolizes the meeting time with her opinions or problems.
- Make every effort to begin and end on time. Pastors' wives are busy people and need this courtesy of the meeting staying within predetermined time limits.

As you think through guidelines in your initial gathering, consider effective groups you've been in and add to the above guidelines as you think helpful.

In conclusion, I believe Gail MacDonald was right in calling the role of pastor's wife a "high call, high privilege." I salute you who, along with your husbands, serve the local church, God's plan for reconciling a lost world to Himself.

---

*I *know* not all pastors are men. There are pastors' husbands — even a handful in my denomination. I'm not discriminating against them in writing to pastors' wives. I simply don't feel qualified to speak to their unique issues.

Contents

INTRODUCTION

PART 1 Relating to God: A Seeker & Finder
    Chapter 1: The Only *Really* Imperative Thing 11
    Chapter 2: An Attitude of Gratitude. 21
    Chapter 3: Ever Feel Disconnected from God?. . . . 31
    Chapter 4: Following Jesus the Hard Way 43
    Chapter 5: The Effective Habit of Plodding 53
    Chapter 6: When Your Reality Check Bounces. . . . 63

PART 2 Relating to Self: Solid at the Center
    Chapter 7: What's Your Worth?. 75
    Chapter 8: Making Change 85
    Chapter 9: Filling Up When You're
               Running on Empty 95
    Chapter 10: Mending Stress Fractures 105
    Chapter 11: Finding Time 117
    Chapter 12: Life's Second Half. 131

PART 3 Relating to Family: An Example of Truth & Grace
    Chapter 13: When Criticism about *Him*
               Hurts You 145
    Chapter 14: Mothering Can Make You
               Hurt All Over 155
    Chapter 15: Hurting Moms Speak Out. 165
    Chapter 16: Love, Honor, & Set Good Boundaries 175

PART 4 **Relating to Ministry: A One-of-a-Kind Servant of God**

    Chapter 17: Have You Joined the Church?...... 191

    Chapter 18: Going on a Niche Hunt 201

    Chapter 19: Signing Up to Have an Impact 209

    Chapter 20: The Gift of a Second Chance 219

    Chapter 21: Close (Staff) Encounters of the Complex Kind.................. 227

PART 5 **Relating to Others: Wise as Serpent, Harmless as Dove**

    Chapter 22: An Interview on Friendship 239

    Chapter 23: 10 Friendship Facts.............. 251

    Chapter 24: Avoiding Mouth Traps 261

    Chapter 25: Is It a Backpack or Burden?........ 271

    Chapter 26: Help That Doesn't Harm People.... 281

    Chapter 27: Is the Woman Driving You Crazy? .. 291

A Concluding Note

    Chapter 28: The View from Retirement 303

Part 1

Relating to God: A Seeker & Finder

1

The Only Really Imperative Thing

Blaise Pascal, a 17th century French physicist and philosopher, wrote, "There is a God-shaped vacuum in the heart of every person that cannot be satisfied by any created thing, but only by God the Creator made known in Jesus Christ."

We evangelicals read that statement and nod our head in agreement. For us, it's creed. Still, that doesn't mean you and I never experience a restless sense of emptiness. That often happens when we fail to take into account that only God can fill a God-space.

I've been contemplating the hurried and harried behavior of many women, and my attention keeps returning to the story of Mary and Martha in Luke 10:38-42. The account is familiar. Jesus was at Martha's house. Maybe because it was her house, Martha felt more responsible for the way it ran. So while Mary sat listening at Jesus' feet — hanging on to His every word as if it were a matter of life and death — Martha was cooking in the kitchen.

Duty Can Kill Delight

I wouldn't be surprised if some of us identify more with Martha and perhaps secretly are attracted more to her than to her sister. Marthas, after all, get things done; they keep projects on course, and pull off events. No doubt about that.

But they can be some of the crabbier people we deal with. Luke's account reveals that the longer Martha spent up to her elbows in dishes and pots, the more upset she got. She felt frustrated, without joy in her labor. She sensed loneliness in the kitchen as she did her duty, but at least she was doing her duty — which was more than she could say of Mary. Frustration, loneliness, and resentment eventually boiled into anger, and Martha's anger was at Jesus.

So she stormed into the living room, glared at Jesus and said, "Lord, *don't you care...*?" Get that? She questioned Jesus' love for her. If He really cared, then surely not for a minute would He tolerate the inconvenience, the inconsiderateness, and the unmitigated unfairness poor Martha was suffering.

"Lord, don't you care that *my sister...*" Don'cha love that? She didn't say "Mary" but "my sister." Kind of reminds me of how angry moms address their kids. When "Pam" became "Pamela L'Nor Hoover!" I knew my mother meant business! "Lord, don't you care that my sister has left me to do all the work by myself? Tell her to help me!"

Martha's focus was on doing her duty, and it's easy to feel alone and angry when your focus is on service to the exclusion of the One you're serving. Doing one's duty for God doesn't produce delight unless it's in the context of experiencing the peaceful intimacy of a love relationship with God. Duty is a poor substitute for enjoying God and serving out of love.

Is Jesus Friend or Guest?

Jesus responded, "Martha, Martha, you are worried and upset about many things, *but only one thing is needed*. Mary has chosen what is better, and it will not be taken away from her."

As I revisited this story a few months ago, I had a new thought. I wondered what would have happened if Martha hadn't treated Jesus like a guest who needed to stay in the living room. I wish she would have dealt with Him as a friend and invited Him into her kitchen. I wondered why she thought she couldn't ask Him to help, or at least watch, her dice onions or cube the meat while they talked of deep and meaningful things.

I'm sure Jesus loved both Mary and Martha and appreciated visiting them. I'm sure as far as Jesus was concerned both Mary and Martha had the option of engaging in the one needed thing of sitting at His feet. I'm also confident that if Martha had sat at Jesus' feet, a meal would have made it to the table eventually.

How Jesus Did It All

I believe this because Jesus showed us that giving priority to spending time with the Father makes life more, not less, productive. Nobody in history accomplished more in three years than Jesus did. He single-handedly defeated death, sin, and Satan; and He provided redemption for all the people of all the world for all time. In addition, during His public ministry, He healed the sick, exorcised evil spirits, fed the hungry, raised the dead, and had a tremendous teaching ministry. He was busy, all right.

But one refrain comes through again and again. We note it in Luke 5:15-16: "Crowds of people came to hear Him and to be healed of their sicknesses. But Jesus often withdrew to places of solitude and prayed." The demands of work never took precedence over spending time alone with His Father.

As I read the Gospels, the pace Jesus kept never vicariously exhausts me. I don't get the feeling He dashed through life with a hassled demeanor and a stressed look on His face in the fashion of us Type A personalities. To me He appears steady, balanced, productive, and unruffled. I think He moved through life like this because He, who fulfilled the Law, fulfilled the command of Psalm 46:10: "Be still, and know that I am God."

Gifts from the Heart

That's what Mary chose when she sat at Jesus' feet that day in Bethany. I suspect because of that she became like Him — steady, balanced, productive, and unruffled. I like to think Martha became like that also because she learned the importance of sitting at Jesus' feet.

On another occasion Jesus visited Bethany (John 12:1-3). Martha served the dinner given in His honor while Mary did a typically Mary thing — she anointed His feet with expensive perfume. I like to think that Martha gave her gift of food to Jesus with the same heart that Mary gave her gift of pure nard. The two sisters were different in many ways. I like to think, however, that each in her own way loved Jesus deeply and did according to her gifts and personality because each had spent quality time with Him.

We women in North America at the beginning of the 21st century have an advantage the two sisters didn't have in their times with Jesus. We know about and have experienced the reality of Jesus' death, resurrection, and ascension. We have the written Old and New Testaments and the indwelling Holy

Spirit. Because of Scripture and Spirit, we can spend a lifetime at Jesus' feet rather than the occasional few hours when He's in the neighborhood.

I challenge you to take time — deliberately, intentionally, consistently — to sit alone in Jesus' presence. Only one thing is needful, so choose the better over the good and the best over the better.

For Personal Meditation & Group Discussion

1. Try this experiment. Every morning ask God to prompt you to have a quiet time (Phil. 2: 13). Expect the Holy Spirit to whisper, "Now!" in your ear. When He speaks, stop everything to spend some minutes with Him. If you disobey His prompting, confess your sin and again open yourself to His still small voice inviting you to come away with Him.

2. Use any or all of the following suggestions for spending time with God.
   - Put a Bible verse over your sink, on your bathroom mirror, or in your car. Say it aloud and meditate on it when you see it.
   - Take a praise walk, thanking God the whole time you're walking outdoors.
   - Prayerfully sing a worship song to God as you work at home or drive to pick up the kids.
   - Keep devotional books in various rooms in your house and in your car and read them when you have a few minutes.
   - Spend a day in personal retreat. Take your Bible, journal, and worship tapes. If at home, turn the phone ringer off.
   - Do a dance to worship music to express your thoughts and feelings to God.
   - Read Eugene Peterson's Bible translation, *The Message,* to hear God's Word afresh.

3. Try practicing *lectio divina* or contemplative Bible reading. The four aspects of this listening for God's voice are:
   - *Listening:* Read a passage of Scripture (it may be short) until you are stopped by a word or phrase that stands out to you. (Some find it helpful to read aloud.) This is what the Spirit is drawing to your attention.
   - *Meditating:* Repeat (aloud or silently) the words or phrase that has grabbed your attention. Consider why these words strike a chord in you. What may God be saying about a situation, question, concern, confusion, need, pain you're experiencing? (Some meditate best by writing thoughts in a journal.)
   - *Praying:* Talk to God about the insights He gives you. Thank Him for speaking. Ask for help to put truth into practice. Claim forgiveness for any sin of which He's made you aware. Praise Him. Be sensitive to the ways God leads you to pray. (Again, you may want to write your prayers in a journal.)
   - *Contemplating:* As you stop talking to God, be silent before Him. Simply be with God. Focus only on the awareness that He is present with and to you. Rest in His nearness. Have an attitude of listening. If your mind wanders, refocus on the words or phrase. As you end this quiet time, go back to your duties with a consciousness that you are in God's loving, guiding presence.

   If you're meeting in a group, take a passage of Scripture (perhaps Luke 8:40-56). Each of you get alone for 20 minutes to do this exercise, and then come back to the group and share your experience of connecting with God.

Dear Friend,

News flash! We can't assume that pastors, their spouses, and Christian leaders spend solid time alone with God regularly. We "professional holy people" know how negligent we can be about what is often termed personal devotions or quiet time.

The church I grew up in expected members to read their Bibles and pray daily. We were encouraged to read through the Bible, so I did. (Leviticus and Ezekiel were a bit much for a kid.) What I'm saying is that there's never been any question about the value of quiet time for me.

That's not to say I've won a gold star for sterling time in Scripture and prayer every day of my life. I remember a period when life seemed just too full. Taking time to sit down appeared impossible, with all I had to do each day. One day I tossed a quasi-apology — in reality a justification for my negligence — God's way: "You know how busy I am."

"You got the dishes done today, didn't you?" the voice in my head asked.

"So?" said I. "They had to be done."

"You made your bed today?" I had — and felt pretty proud about it too!

"Let Me see if I'm getting this straight. A tidy house has far higher priority than nurturing your relationship with Me?"

"Well, if You put it *that* way," I pouted. Then conviction hit.

My priorities really were out of kilter. I realized mastering my to-do list every day wasn't going to get me a crown in heaven. I wasn't getting much reward on earth either, come to think of it, except the praise of my compulsive ego.

I've spent decades now trying to simplify my life and set priorities in order to spend quality time with God. When I take time to be with Him, I experience more serenity and productivity and less frantic hyperactivity.

Augustine wrote, "You have created us for Yourself, O God, and our hearts are restless until they rest in You." I pray you'll find the rest that comes by daily letting God fill up the God-space in you.

Warmly,

Pamela

2
An Attitude of Gratitude

My husband and I took our daughter to the zoo the other day. It so happened they were giving away candy treats. I noticed that Faith was the only child who said, "Thank you." (I was also the only parent I heard prompting her child with the question, "What do you say?")

"No one enjoys hanging around an ingrate," wrote Sarah Ban Breathnach in her best-selling *Simple Abundance.* Yet saying thank you may be the hardest of good manners to learn. Many adults, who chew food with their lips closed and cover their sneezes and coughs, blow it in the gratitude department.

Mark Twain cynically observed, "If you pick up a starving dog and make him prosperous, he will not bite you; that is the principal difference between a dog and a man." That's generally an overstatement; most of us aren't so much guilty of returning meanness for kindness as we are of simply failing to note the kindnesses that come our way, or maybe of thinking we have a right to what we get. Perhaps we just believe in error that others know we're thankful without our saying so.

The Score: 9 to 1

When John wrote his Gospel, he said that Jesus did and said numerous things during His time on earth. In fact, He did so much that only some of His deeds were recorded; it would have been too daunting a task to write down every action and word of Jesus.

With that in mind, I've read the Gospels with the question, "Of all that Jesus said and did, why did the Holy Spirit inspire the writers of Scripture to include *this* incident?" My thinking is that if a particular account "made the editorial cut," then it contains something of vital importance for us to know. That's why the story of the ten lepers grabs my attention as being of particular significance.

Luke 17:11-19 tells us that ten lepers approached Jesus. Their deadly contagion, unlike that of HIV-positive people, could be spread by casual contact. That's why lepers were outcasts from the society. Wherever they went, they had to yell, "Unclean!" to warn others to give them wide berth lest they contaminate others.

No wonder, then, that the lepers sought healing when they heard a miracle-worker was in the vicinity. "Jesus, Master, have mercy on us," they cried. Jesus had mercy and cured them.

One man, realizing he'd been healed, returned to Jesus and thanked Him profusely. The Divine Doctor asked, "Weren't ten cleansed? Where are the other nine? Why have none come back to give God glory except for this foreigner?" (The grateful one was a Samaritan, a person definitely low on the rungs of the social ladder in Israel.)

Perhaps the other healed lepers felt entitled. After all, they were God's chosen, the children of Abraham. Maybe they felt they deserved what they got, that healing was their right rather than a tremendous gift. If so, expressing gratitude may never have entered their craniums.

Even Secular Affirmation

One of the popular spiritual emphases in current American culture, espoused even in the secular arena, is consistent with biblical truth — the value of gratitude.

Thus, one can tune in to Oprah's television talk show and hear her urge viewers to count their blessings and record them daily. In a secular bookstore one can buy *The Simple Abundance Journal of Gratitude*, which provides pages for recording five blessings each day for which one is thankful. Implicit in all this is the realization that daily we receive gifts worth noticing and appreciating, gifts that come from "a Higher Power," "Spirit," or whatever secular people recognize as Something Transcendent. We Christians say gifts come from the God of the Bible.

Those touting the practice of noting and recording the good things that come our way each day claim this practice benefits people. We become, they say, more peaceful and content. We experience a greater sense of well-being and joy. This emphasis on being thankful is recommended because of what a grateful heart gains us personally, not necessarily on our reasonable obligation to honor the Giver of the gifts.

We Owe Thankfulness

Beyond what gratitude does for us, the Bible is clear on the fact that giving thanks is an act of obedience. Christians are commanded in Ephesians 5:20 and 1 Thessalonians 5:19 to give thanks in and for all things. A grateful heart apparently is of great value to God. It doesn't take too much imagination and reasoning to understand why this may be so.

First, gratitude for God's blessings shows that we understand the source of every good and perfect gift (James 1:17). After we've done all we can to act responsibly in regard to diet, rest, and exercise, we still know that God is the source of strength, health, and life. Though we may gather facts and study the pros and cons of a situation prior to making a decision, we recognize the limits of our information and our need of God's wisdom. While we give due consideration to developing our character, we realize that in the flesh we can't successfully overcome the temptation to sin; without the Holy Spirit's empowerment, we will fail. Indeed God is not a nicety; He is our very necessity. Without Him we can do nothing, we have nothing, we are little more than grass that is here today and gone tomorrow. Thankful people have grasped that.

Second, gratitude for God's blessings expresses faith in Him. This is especially true in praising Him in the difficult times we face. When we thank God in the midst of life's troubles, we declare our trust that He still loves us and exercises His power and wisdom on our behalf regardless of any appearance to the contrary. Some thank offerings really are a sacrifice; they cost us dearly because they are expressed with tears through confusion, disappointment, pain, and grief. Praise transcends the temporal, reminding us that eternal goodness and mercy is ours in Jesus Christ.

A Blessing Catcher

As Christians we've often been encouraged to write down and date our prayer requests in a notebook. We've been told to record answers to those prayers so we properly give God due credit. That's all well and good, but perhaps we need to do more and have "a blessing catcher" notebook.

Daily we receive answered un-prayers (as opposed to unanswered prayers); we are gifted with blessings it may never have occurred to us to ask for. A spectacular sunrise or sunset. A good bargain at the market. A friend's encouragement. Savory aromas of food cooking or baking. A child's impulsive hug. Even a flowering weed. A kind word.

To cultivate an attitude of gratitude is to be on the alert for God's presence in our ordinary experience of everyday life. To watch consciously for the sprinkling of God's blessings throughout the course of our day makes us aware of divine activity, in little as well as large things, in our common routines. That alertness, that awareness of occasions for thankfulness, becomes a way of practicing the presence of God. To that end, may we nurture a spirit of appreciation that turns our minds and hearts Godward in the midst of even humdrum activity.

For Personal Meditation & Group Discussion

1. Consider how you can apply the following quotations about thanksgiving.

   a. "A thankful heart is not only the greatest virtue, but the parent of all other virtues" (Cicero).

   b. "It is always possible to be thankful for what is given rather than to complain about what is not given. One or the other becomes a habit of life" (Elizabeth Elliot).

   c. "Be on the lookout for mercies. The more we look for them, the more of them we will see. Blessings brighten when we count them. Better to lose count while naming your blessings than to lose your blessings by counting your troubles" (Maltbie Babcock).

   d. "Praise is like a plow set to go deep into the soil of believers' hearts. It lets the glory of God into the details of daily living" (C. M. Hanson).

   e. Matthew Henry, after being robbed: "I thank Thee first because I was never robbed before; second, because although they took my purse they did not take my life; third, although they took my all, it was not much; and fourth, because it was I who was robbed and not I who robbed."

2. Read Psalms 107 and 136. Underline the recurring phrase in each psalm. Do you see any significance in this repetition?

3. According to Philippians 4:6, what is an antidote to anxious thoughts and feelings? How does this apply specifically in your ministry life?

4. According to Colossians 3:17, what is our underlying attitude to be in all our ministries to others in Jesus' name? Why is this important when we're the givers rather than the receivers?

Dear Friend!

For a time during his high school years, our son took all the good things we did for him for granted. He was remarkably mature in many ways. He wasn't rebellious. He didn't smart-mouth us. He brought his friends home by the droves and seemed proud of his family. But his attitude of entitlement drove me up a wall and sometimes over it. Maybe it was the very goodness of his behavior that caused him to think he deserved a week at camp, to drive our car, and not to have to work to pay for his own car insurance. More likely this attitude was due to temporary teenage insanity. In any case, we had many a conversation about this.

Both people who grow up with a lot and those who grow up with little can have a sense of entitlement. Even if they don't say it, a current can run through their soul that life owes them good stuff.

Christians, being your common ordinary people, can have that same perspective. Those of us who serve God can even consciously or unconsciously hold the belief that God owes us. After all, look what we have given up or put up with to obey Him! Then when we get what we feel we deserve, we don't receive it with a grateful heart.

Some of us lack gratitude simply because we haven't taken time to cultivate our awareness of the small kindnesses, the unexpected serendipities, or even the significant blessings that come our way. Sometimes we have to lose a long string of sunny days, our health, or a meaningful relationship to realize the value of ordinary good gifts.

When my daughter was in preschool, her teacher spent a week talking about good manners. The focus wasn't on the fine points of holding a fork correctly or not asking nosy questions. This was strictly about the most basic etiquette — saying *please* and *thank you*.

I'm glad for the reinforcement the teacher gave us in teaching Faith good manners. She's getting better at saying thank you. I appreciate how often I hand her something and hear, "Thanks, Mommy." Still, I find I have to remind her almost every day to say thank you. But then I have to remind myself often to express gratitude to my Abba for the thousand and one things I take for granted.

As you do an attitude check, how's your gratitude? How do you cultivate it?

I remain thankful for you. I thank God that you serve Him, that together we're part of His Family, and that He's given me the privilege of connecting with you.

Gratefully,

Pamela

3
Ever Feel Disconnected From God?

Every Christian has times when she feels she's lost God's phone number. Or she dials but can't get through. She longs to hear His voice, but her seeming inability to make contact shakes her sense of spiritual security. I'm not just talking about specific prayers not being answered as quickly or in the way we'd like. The feeling is a more generalized sense that connection with God is lost.

Various saints of old have called this experience the dark night of the soul, the silence of God, and spiritual dryness. "The Sahara of the soul" is Richard Foster's term for it (*Prayer: Finding the Heart's True Home*).

However we label it, it can be uncomfortable and unsettling. We fear it signals spiritual failure on our part. Or that it's going to last forever.

Part of the Rhythm

I once heard a pastor give three reasons why believers find themselves in this situation: apathy toward God, disobeying His commands, and resenting His allowances in their lives. Each of these causes indicates sin on our part which, indeed, can result in spiritual flatness.

Spiritual dryness, however, may have nothing to do with sin. As Foster wrote, it "does not mean that God is displeased with you, or that you are insensitive to the work of God's Spirit, or that you have committed some horrendous offense against heaven.... *Darkness is to be expected, even embraced* (emphasis mine)."

C. S. Lewis knew that sometimes God allows His children to have a strong sense of His presence, *but...*

> He never allows this state of affairs to last long. Sooner or later He withdraws, if not in fact, at least from their conscious experience, all those supports and incentives. He allows the creature to stand up on its own legs — to carry out from the will alone duties which lost all relish. It is during such trough periods, much more than during the peak periods, that it is growing into the sort of creature He wants it to be (*The Screwtape Letters*).

John Ortberg says spiritual highs and lows are a matter of inevitability — troughs are as certain in the life of faith as are the peaks. In his book, *The Life You've Always Wanted*, he wrote: "One of the basic laws of life is rhythm. Night follows day, winter follows summer.... In spiritual life, the traditional language for this is rhythm. There will be times of consolation and times of desolation."

Maybe I'm Sinning

I didn't understand this when I was 21. I had trusted Christ as Savior as a child and took my faith seriously even through my teens. I'd established a habit of regular quiet times and committed myself for Christian service. I knew what it was to feel close to my heavenly Father. But during my senior year in college I got a bad case of the spiritual blahs.

God felt far away. Bible reading was flat; praying seemed a fruitless ritual. Foster could have been describing me when he wrote, "We question, we doubt, we struggle. We pray and the words feel rote. We turn to the Bible and find it meaningless. We turn to music and it fails to move us."

Ortberg would say I was in the desolation phase of the rhythm of spiritual life: "In times of consolation we like to pray because God seems close, the Bible seems alive, sin looks bad, and stoplights all seem green. Times of desolation are just the opposite: The Bible seems dry, prayer grows hard, and God is far away."

Feeling emotionally distant from God, I was anything but apathetic toward Him. I felt deeply distressed; so much so that it sucked the joy out of my life. Tears came easily as I assumed that I must be sinning in some horrible way I couldn't pinpoint.

I tried all the remedies I knew of. I looked for sins to confess. Hadn't I had often read, "Your sins have hidden his face from you" (Isaiah 59:2)? I repented of everything I thought might possibly be wrong in my life, but still I felt an uneasy spiritual malaise. I read Scripture hoping for some truth to cure me, but the Great Physician seemed far away.

Maybe I'm Just Plain Tired

As I look back on that time from today's perspective, I

might think I was simply due for a time in the valley. Or it could also be true that I was simply feeling the exhaustion of a new bride in the unaccustomed role of taking care of a home, studying to maintain an A average at Nyack College, and working part-time to bring in some money. Tiredness as the possible cause aside, a valuable insight finally broke through.

One day I was praying and full of introspection about what awful thing I might be doing to be reaping such a harvest. Then it dawned on me that if sin were the reason I felt so dry, then it was the Holy Spirit's job to reveal it. Jesus had called the Spirit my Convicter. I could count on Him to show me if I were out of fellowship with God. That truth marked the beginning of several lessons the Father would teach me through the years about dealing with vague guilt feelings that attach to false guilt and the depressing affects of the performance trap bequeathed to me by my legalistic church background.

Maybe I'm Useless

A couple of years later, I again felt spiritually low. I'd committed my life to serve Jesus as a child. That dedication expressed itself in my going to a Christian college to prepare myself for ministry. After graduation I went forth eagerly to do whatever God had for me to do in the new city in the new part of the country where He'd led my husband and me. Despite my enthusiasm and desire to serve Jesus, I sensed doors of ministry were more closed than open. The discouraging, scary thought crossed my mind that God didn't consider me usable.

I waited for divine guidance but received the "silence of God." I didn't get the affirmation I sought — that God really had called me to serve Him and had a place for me in ministry. That came months later. In the meantime, He seemed far off.

He definitely didn't seem to be in my tiny Midwestern home — hadn't been for days and weeks.

Since misery loves company, one day I opened to the book of Job to have a good pity party along with another who also wondered where God was. Job said,

> If only I knew where to find him; if only I could go to his dwelling!... But if I go to the east, he is not there; if I go to the west, I do not find him. When he is at work in the north, I do not see him; when he turns to the south, I catch no glimpse of him. But he knows the way that I take; when he has tested me, I will come forth as gold (Job 23:3, 8-10).

He knows the way that I take. I held on to that truth white-knuckled! My security lies in the fact that God always knows exactly where I am. I'm not hidden to Him even when He feels hidden to me. He's there whether or not I sense His presence, whether He speaks or remains silent.

The Reality of Relationships

Ask yourself as I have, Do I have any relationship in which I always feel warmly, wonderfully, vitally, totally connected?

My answer is, of course not! The pattern is one of ebb and flow. I have a nice husband, an affectionate and fun child, some good friends, a fine extended family, and a wonderful team of ministry colleagues. I love them and they love me, and all's well in my world. The tide is high. Sometimes, however, I don't sense warmth, delight and connection with them. Though I know that our love, respect, and commitment for each other are firm, the tide is definitely out. So, I've learned not to base my horizontal relationships on feelings.

And I don't base my vertical relationship with God on emotions either. Some days I don't sense God's love or presence.

Perhaps I have a cold. Or I'm confused about something, and He isn't giving me an answer. Or I'm in emotional pain, and His healing comfort isn't taking it away. Or traveling has made me beyond exhausted. Such feelings often cause me also to feel flat, dry, cold spiritually.

That emotional state doesn't mean God isn't cherishing me and closer to me than my breath. His care and nearness are indisputable; His Word assures me that He never forsakes me. He loves me with an everlasting love — even when I feel unattractive, unlovable, out of sorts, worthless, and clueless. Even when He seems silent and absent.

Benefits of the Dark Times

A friend once told me, "Sometimes the Christian life is like shredded wheat. It's dry, but good for you." What's the good in the dry times?

First, dry times force us to live by faith and not by sight. Jesus told Thomas, "Because you have seen me, you have believed; blessed are those who have not seen and yet have believed" (John 20:29). Jesus sees faith that doesn't depend on constant validation as superior, more mature faith.

Let's be honest — we don't suffer winters by choice. Were the decision ours, we would always opt to have warm, intimate feelings of connectedness to God. Lacking that, however, we needn't go into a tailspin when we have to walk by faith in His promises and not by a pleasant feeling that are wrapped in His embrace.

Second, feeling lonely for God prompts us to seek Him. I believe that what hunger is to eating and thirst is to drinking, spiritual homesickness is to moving us toward God. When we feel uneasy about a relationship, we tend to reevaluate its priority in our lives and give it more attention.

Still, we must remember God is not a divine automatic teller machine whom we can manipulate by inserting the right card and punching in the correct personal identification number. Even if we intensify our focus on God, that doesn't mean He's obligated to speak, shed light, melt the ice, or send refreshing showers. The spiritual life is never a matter of figuring out how to "work" God to get the desired answer to prayer or emotional payback.

God is the sovereign Alpha and Omega. He is the Author and the Finisher of our faith — and everything between the beginning and the end. He moves according to His own timetable and purposes.

Third, feeling far from God can correct wrong assumptions about who He is and how He relates to His children. God has a way of not allowing us to confine Him to our tidy little boxes of how He does or must act. Foster wrote, "God, the great iconoclast, is constantly smashing our false images of who he is and what he is like… God is slowly weaning us of fashioning him in our own image."

So many how-to books are available to us. Some of them give us four easy steps to trusting Christ or six steps to being filled with His Spirit or eight steps to victory over temptation. A lot of truth may be contained in those books. When it's all said and done, however, God and our life of faith cannot be fit into neat little packages. God has a way of working outside precise categories of how He can, does, or must work.

So, in the dry times we cling to our personal relationship with Him. We cling in trust whether we feel better or worse, richer or poorer, sick or healthy, rested or tired, calm or stressed, stale or exciting, attractive or ugly — you get the point. When it's dry, we hang on in hope until He sends showers once again. Our role is to take time to be quiet before Him, opening ourselves to listen for His voice. We walk by faith.

For Personal Meditation & Group Discussion

1. Jesus called Himself the Light of the world. But "He made darkness His covering, His canopy around Him — the dark rain clouds of the sky" (Ps. 18:11). Think about what it means that God created both light *and* darkness.

2. Read what a man after God's own heart wrote in Psalm 13:1-6. What other biblical characters had similar experiences? Tell about your own experience.

3. What do you think about the following quotes:
   - "No natural feelings are high or low, holy or unholy, in themselves. They are all holy when God's hand is on the rein" (C. S. Lewis).
   - "Turn your doubts to questions; turn your questions to prayers; turn your prayers to God" (Mark R. Littleton).

4. Psalm 18:28 says, "You, O Lord, keep my lamp burning; my God turns my darkness into light." How do you maintain such hope when the darkness lasts longer than you like?

5. Reflect on Lamentations 3:6-26. What's your definition of hope? Where do you think you rate on the hope scale right now?

6. Can you relate a time when you were scared in physical darkness, but found comfort in another's presence? Then read Deuteronomy 31:8 and apply that to the dark night of the soul.

Dear Friend,

I don't know about you, but I rarely hear people confess to spiritual dryness.

Maybe we good Christian women don't talk about the times God seems silent because we fear we'll damage some weaker Christian by acknowledging that even mature believers can hit an arid patch. After all, don't we sometimes "sell" the gospel with the promise of a fulfilling, personal, never-ending relationship with Jesus?

Maybe we keep our drought hidden because we fear such an admission would bring on criticism and judgment: "Is there sin in your life?" "Are you consistent in having quiet times?" "Where's your faith?"

I'm writing this less than a week after the Holy Week's remembrance of Jesus' experience in Gethsemane prior to His crucifixion. Was the darkness of the garden that night matched by the internal darkness the Son of God felt? I believe His anguished cry from the cross — "My God! My God! Why have You forsaken Me?" — expressed a profound and real sense of the Father's absence. The dark night of His soul was externalized in the darkness that covered the land from noon until 3 p.m. And Jesus perfectly fulfilled the Father's will.

That gives us a clue that despite our discipline in spending quality time with God, we're only one part of the relationship. God is the other part, and His part is the greater one. That means you and I can be faithful in reading Scripture, praying, meditating and journaling, serving Him and others, and walking by means of the Spirit, and still go through times of spiritual drought. At such times, you may feel frustrated, look for reasons. Perhaps the explanation is simply that God has entrusted you with a time of "Sahara of the soul" for His own good reasons. Maybe it's time for you to learn to see in the dark.

How do you survive the desert? Richard Foster makes this suggestion for our dark and dry times:

> We may not see the end from the beginning, but we keep on doing what we know to do. We pray, we listen, we worship, we carry out the duty of the present moment. What we learned to do in the light of God's love, we also do in the dark of God's absence. We ask and continue to ask, even though there is no answer. We seek and continue to seek, even though we do not find. We knock, and continue to knock, even though the door remains shut.
>
> This constant, longing love produces a firmness of life orientation in us. We love God more than the gifts God brings. Like Job, we serve God even if he slays us. Like Mary, we say freely, "I am the Lord's servant. May it be to me as You have said" (Luke 1:38).

I've memorized this for my dark-night times.

Warmly,

Pamela

4
Following Jesus the Hard Way

My flight was scheduled for around 11:30 that morning, allowing me to get dressed and out the door at a more leisurely pace than I'm used to. About 8 o'clock, however, stomach pains and nausea hit suddenly. I writhed in bed and made quick trips to the bathroom. All the while I was thinking, *I have to get to Iowa to speak at that retreat.*

Being the spiritual giant I am (Ha!), I was also thinking, *OK, God, I'm committed to expressing Your grace and truth to women this weekend. Wouldn't You call this bad timing for flu, a touch of food poisoning, or whatever? I do Your work, and You allow this? This stinks!* (Honest confession may be good for my soul, but it's lousy for the reputation.)

With *great* effort, I finally threw some clothes on and made a pass at making up my face. Enroute to the airport, my husband stopped at Safeway so I could ask the pharmacist the best over-the-counter medication to stop vomiting. I held on to that bottle all day with the passion of a wino with his booze. I arrived at the retreat feeling like roadkill looks (maybe also looking like roadkill looks). Those good women of Iowa prayed over me, and the first message somehow got out of my mouth that evening. Thankfully, after a night's rest I felt much better the next day.

Call it spiritual warfare if you wish, but the fact remains that God didn't make serving Him in Iowa easy that weekend.

Isn't It Supposed to Be Easier?

Have you heard that life will be smooth for Christians who have enough faith and no unconfessed sin in their lives? While you and I reject name-it-and-claim-it (AKA blab-it-and-grab-it!) theology, many of us have been infected with the unhealthy idea that life in the center of God's will should make for smooth sailing in the rough seas of a sin-cursed world. This despite Jesus' warning that suffering is on the charts for us.

I think of a pastor's wife who wrote a while back about her struggle with the church's shabby treatment of her husband. "I know for a fact that he is the best thing that ever happened to this church, but somehow the fact has escaped some of the people." The result was suffering for her and her family. She, like many of us, has discovered that saying "Yes!" to God's call is often easier than living "Yes!" But then it's always been that way.

After Moses responded to God's call and set off for Egypt to lead the Israelites out of slavery, it went downhill. Pharaoh did not look favorably on that venture and made life even harder for the Israelites. They turned on Moses, telling him he'd be the death of them! No wonder Moses complained (Exod. 5:22), "O Lord, why have you brought trouble upon this people? Is this why you sent me?" As we'd say today, it didn't figure — Moses did what God told him to, and life got tough.

Centuries later God called Jeremiah, promising him, "Do not be afraid… for I am with you and will rescue you.… I have put My words in your mouth… I appoint you over nations and kingdoms to uproot and tear down, to destroy and overthrow, to build and to plant" (Jer. 1:8-10). The man wound up in a cistern, standing in muck and yuck. Feeling blindsided by God, He charged, "O Lord, you deceived me, and I was deceived; you overpowered me and prevailed" (20:7). Somewhere I read that "you seduced me and then raped me" is more in the spirit of the Hebrew.

Mary's Experience

And what could have been more painful than the experience of the mother of Jesus? God undoubtedly called Mary to incubate His Son within her womb — her conceiving as a virgin gave proof positive of God's will. Yet her soul was lacerated again and again.

Mary had to travel long miles from Nazareth to Bethlehem in the last stages of her pregnancy. Riding a donkey or walking, either way it couldn't have been a picnic. She gave birth in a barn and probably her mother wasn't there to assist in the delivery. Within hours a bunch of sheep-smelly strangers, responding to the angels' song, trouped into the "bedroom" of the exhausted new mother, barely more than a girl.

Mary and her husband weren't rich. They offered the poor person's sacrifice of two doves at the purification ceremony. The comfort of material goods didn't smooth their life situation.

Mary knew the trauma of moving to a foreign country with her toddler, away from familiar people, language, and customs.

(Like if I went to live in Italy.) Even at a distance she may have heard of the deaths of children, whose mothers she may have known, and grieved their execution. Do you think she ever thought, 'How can God let me go through this when I risked sabotaging my upcoming marriage and certainly my reputation in being pregnant on my wedding day?'

Mary's other children didn't believe in their Brother until after the resurrection. I suppose her young sons were as prone to sibling rivalry as kids are today. I can hear them taunting, "Jesus, you act so perfect you make me sick." And Mary had to referee these skirmishes.

Nothing prepared Mary for the reality of Jesus' public ministry. He spent his time with the "wrong" people, alienating the respected Jewish religious leaders. At one point, the family was convinced He was out of control, and they sought to make an intervention. Ultimately, Mary saw the will of God for her accused, tried, condemned, mocked, tortured, and crucified. She had a front row seat at the quintessential hate crime of all history, and the victim was her *son*.

On this side of Easter we have to work hard to empathize with what it meant for Mary to live Maundy Thursday, how-can-I-call-it-*Good*? Friday, and dead-Dead-DEAD! Saturday. What wails did she send heavenward between His arrest that Thursday night and her despairing walk to the tomb as Sunday dawned? It wouldn't take much for me to believe that the young teen's "I am the Lord's servant… May it be to me as you have said" (Luke 1:38) became "This is what being your handmaiden gets me? I devote myself to your Son, and you let him be killed? Have I missed something here? My son is dead, and that's *not* OK with me!"

Who Are You, God?

Perhaps nothing tests our trust in God as does suffering. Suffering by definition is miserable, whether it's illness, chronic pain, church conflict, broken relationships, death of a loved one, or financial stress. For many of us, however, the worst part is the spiritual suffering that easily attaches to the physical and emotional. Spiritual suffering raises questions such as: Why doesn't God answer my prayers? What kind of God is He not to respond to my need or to intervene in this evil situation? Shouldn't following God's will mean gates opening on to smooth highways? Is this happening because I'm out of His will?

I write this on the one-year anniversary of my darling granddaughter's coming to live with me permanently. For three years I'd observed that she was malnourished and often dirty in an irrational and immoral home. I watched as she experienced one traumatic event and another. I saw the affects of damage to her wee soul. I've never prayed so passionately and persistently as I did for her rescue. And nothing happened. Furthermore, God was silent. I felt confused, hurt, sad, and angry. Still, by God's grace I trusted that His grace was sufficient for me when I didn't feel even a tad spiritual, victorious, or joyful. I simply persevered, hanging on white-knuckled and doing what Richard Foster calls "the duty of the present moment."

In an issue of *Leadership Journal*, Marshall Shelley discussed how the death of his two children affected his view of God and the Christian life. He wrote, "I hadn't realized the cost of discipleship.... Living for God's glory isn't for sissies." He noted some other results: "It's harder to confidently make specific requests.... Prayer is now an intense desire to know God, to understand His ways, and to see good come out of pain." He notes he learned a more intentional faith: "Innocent faith can trust God because it hasn't seen the abyss; virtuous faith has known the terror and chooses to trust God." I identify with Shelley.

I know for sure that God doesn't handle His servants with kid gloves. He doesn't cut ministry wives a better deal because "we have left all to follow you." While I understand this better, I understand some things less. I live with more unanswered questions and greater humility — the glass I see through is darker than I'd thought. A high IQ can't grasp the Immortal.

The Way of the Cross

While reading Philip Yancey's *The Jesus I Never Knew*, I was viscerally struck by the magnitude of the rejection and torture Jesus experienced. He, also, felt abandoned by Almighty God, who didn't lift a finger to put either the Sanhedrin or the Roman soldiers in their place.

Meditating on this, I thought how my prayer throughout my decades as a believer has been to become more Christlike. It dawns on me that to be conformed to the image of Christ probably means suffering. "Not my will but Yours be done" likely will necessitate going to my own personal Gethsamane and Cross so that Christ is formed in me. Probably Almighty God won't pull a dramatic power play to rescue me. I must learn the obedience of faith through suffering.

I think of Philippians 3:10-11. "I want to know Christ and the power of his resurrection and the fellowship of sharing in his sufferings, becoming like him in his death, and so, somehow, to attain to the resurrection from the dead."

Was Paul bonkers? I can understand his wanting to know Jesus. I can understand his longing to know resurrection power.

But wanting to know the fellowship of sharing in Jesus' sufferings? Call me a coward, but I'd just as soon not hurt! And probably most believers hope God's will for us won't include suffering.

I recall that Paul wrote Philippians from prison. By then he'd been through a veritable mountain of suffering. He had an experienced-gained perspective. He saw that sharing in Christ's sufferings had been redemptive for both him and the kingdom.

I'll try to keep that in mind the next time I'm doing God's will and it isn't easy. I'll try to trust God's redemptive purposes even when I can't fathom them. Even when I feel queasy enroute to Iowa.

For Personal Meditation & Group Discussion

1. What evidence can you give that the Sovereign of the universe doesn't tend toward power plays to make life a bed of roses for His people?

2. If suffering isn't the indicator that you're out of God's will, how can you know whether or not you're in line with God's will?

3. If your area of stress is ministry related, think of what it cost Paul to minister (2 Cor. 11:22-29). Then meditate on 1 Corinthians 15:58, Galatians 6:9, Colossians 3:23-24 and 2 Corinthians 4:17-18. What insights have you gained?

4. How do you feel about this prayer? "Teach me, dear God, the glory of my cross; teach me the value of my 'thorn.' Show me that I have climbed to Thee by the path of pain. Show me that my tears have made my rainbow" (George Matheson).

5. Read Philip Yancey's *The Jesus I Never Knew,* especially the part focusing on the suffering of Jesus.

Dear Friend,

As I write this chapter, I'm deeply aware of the stress and distress many pastors' wives are enduring. For example, I got a call from a ministry woman whose husband had been forced to resign. This call came on the heels of learning a church had just fired its senior pastor and refused even to consider mediation to resolve the conflict.

It may be apocryphal, but years ago I heard that Corrie ten Boom was asked about her ministry in the United States. Corrie's beloved father and sister died in a Nazi concentration camp. Corrie herself suffered demeaning trauma as she lived with cold, vermin, starvation, filth, cruelty, and the constant threat of death. So, what was Corrie's mission in our country? As I heard it, she said she'd come to talk to American Christians about suffering. She didn't think we were well prepared to handle it.

How could those of us who lived through communism's closing churches, killing pastors, sending godly parents to Siberian slave camps, and refusing education to their children ever give credence to the idea that suffering doesn't have any part in the Christian life?

So where we do we get the idea that life is supposed to be nice — especially for us who serve Christ? We could blame television preachers. Many seem to camp on the idea that with enough faith God will make us prosperous — financially and otherwise. They're dead wrong, of course.

This chapter refers to biblical giants of the faith who certainly didn't find life easy. Our personal observations confirm that God's servants still don't walk a smooth path to heaven.

I don't like that idea. Neither does my husband who just read this chapter. Biased as he is (even saying I'm aged to perfection), he commented that the material was good and well-written but he added, "I don't like the idea." We don't like suffering even if we like what it has produced.

Maybe that's because God didn't create us for suffering. He made us for something far better — like Eden or heaven. Thousands of years since the Fall, our inner being knows this is not the way it's supposed to be. The Good News is that some day it will no longer be this way. That's the believer's hope. Meanwhile, we keep saying "Yes!" to God's will, trusting that God's plans for us are good.

Warmly,

Pamela

5
The Effective Habit of Plodding

Humorist Josh Billings reminds us that the usefulness of a postage stamp is in sticking to one thing until it gets there. He's talking about plodding step after step until the destination is reached.

William Carey, when asked the reason for his success as a missionary, replied, "I can plod." Indeed, walking until the goal is achieved is at the heart of most vital ministries. At a gathering of pastors, the speaker noted that pastors who stay put in a church for awhile usually accomplish a more significant work than do short-timers.

A Matter of Definition

But let's be honest. Endurance and perseverance are such stodgy words. Dreary fog hangs about them. As virtues, they lack the appeal and brilliance of love and joy and goodness and honesty. Yet the Spirit's fruit of patience, faithfulness, and self-control — qualities connoting persistence and the ability to delay gratification — are central to a full expression of our Christlikeness. Tediousness and tiresomeness, however, aren't the most disturbing aspects of persevering. It's the toughness we resist.

Greek words translated "endurance" and "perseverance" in the New Testament give a broad range of meanings: constancy, to adhere closely to, to continue in, to have fortitude, to patiently suffer, to put up or bear with — especially afflictions and trouble.

The real rub with the whole notion of perseverance is the implication that things don't happen as easily or quickly as we'd like. If we have to endure something, it's painful (eating chocolate isn't a matter of endurance for me); and the human bent is to seek pleasure and avoid pain. We don't eagerly anticipate practicing the virtue of perseverance.

A Drive to Thrive

This morning I read again the parable of the sower. Jesus noted three reasons why the sown seed fails to produce a crop. He said a fruitful harvest comes from seed planted on good soil, that is, "those with a noble and good heart, who hear the word, retain it, and by *persevering* produce a crop" (Luke 8:15, emphasis added). In Jesus' story, the difference between reaping or not reaping spiritually lies in persevering in what we know of the will of God.

When David Sarnoff wrote, "The will to persevere is often the difference between failure and success," in all likelihood he wasn't thinking of our personal spiritual development or our efforts to build the kingdom. Nevertheless, to a great extent whether you and I accomplish "something beautiful for God" (Mother Teresa's words) depends on our passionate persistence in being and doing what He's called us to be and do. That often requires white-knuckled hanging on when we'd rather throw in the towel and walk away.

Even on Blue Mondays

I wonder how many pastors resign on a blue Monday after a rough Sunday.

I attended a gathering in Dallas on the church of the 21st century. Pastor and author Leith Anderson's address to the conferees vulnerably exposed three crucial times when he struggled to continue in ministry. He told of a Sunday afternoon when, after preaching that morning, he sat on his bed and searched the want ads for a job to support his family — this despite his church having significant growth. We understand that, don't we?

We who serve Christ through the church can wrestle with the temptation to quit even when things are going fairly well, because of the nature of our task. In our work we deal with people, and people tend to make ministry messy and stressful. In our work we also struggle "against the spiritual forces of evil in the heavenly realms" (Eph. 6:12), and this warfare is exhausting and bloody. No wonder Paul exhorted Timothy four times in two short letters to persevere and endure hardship (1 Tim. 4:16, 6:11, 2 Tim. 2:3, 4:5).

Exhortations to Us

And the writers of Scripture urge all of us believers to keep on keeping on:

Therefore, since we are surrounded by such a great cloud of witnesses, let us throw off everything that hinders and the sin that so easily entangles, and let us run with perseverance the race marked out for us (Heb. 12:1).

Therefore, my dear [sisters and] brothers, stand firm. Let nothing move you. Always give yourselves fully to the work of the Lord, because you know that your labor in the Lord is not in vain (1 Cor. 15:58).

Let us not become weary in doing good, for at the proper time we will reap a harvest if we do not give up (Gal. 6:9).

What's the Use?

The Bible tells us our stick-to-itiveness is instrumental in sinners' salvation. Paul said he endured everything that the elect might obtain salvation through Jesus (2 Tim. 2:10). He promised that if we persevere in our life and doctrine, "you will save both yourself and your hearers" (1 Tim. 4:16).

The Bible assures us that our passionate persistence not only benefits others but us personally. Paul, Peter, and James all agree that perseverance is part and parcel of the development of Christian character (Rom. 5:2-4, James 1:2-4, 2 Pet. 1:5-8). 1 John 2:28 says when we remain constant, we have confidence before Jesus.

The Bible says that, when we keep our trust in God while enduring difficulties, we encourage others to hope in Jesus (1 Thess. 1:3) Furthermore, our endurance is commendable before God (1 Pet. 2:20). Note how God expressed appreciation for the perseverance of three first-century churches (Rev. 2:2, 2:19, 3:10). Our endurance delights God.

Where Do I Get It?

So we've coped with tough stuff in ministry, but maybe today — or soon — we find ourselves, as a friend expressed it, "fresh out of cope." Where do we get perseverance? When Paul ran into a wall, he learned that the ability to bear up didn't come from himself (2 Cor. 1:8-11). It comes from God (Rom. 15:5-6). "Patient endurance," said John, "is ours in Jesus" (Rev. 1:9).

The Bible records God's working "to teach us, so that through endurance and the encouragement of the Scriptures we might have hope" (Rom. 15:4). As we read the stories of how saints before us, in both Old and New Testaments, ran the race despite significant hardship, we take heart in the midst of our trials. (Have any who accomplished great things for God traveled an easy path?) We immerse ourselves in the promises of the God-there-for-us and the reward for those who remain faithful.

The Bible reveals prayer as powerful to help us endure. Paul credited the prayers of the Corinthians in helping him endure until rescue (2:1:8-11). He prayed for the Colossians to have great endurance (1:9-12). How blessed we are that Jesus and the Spirit intercede for us while a great host of saints who have gone before us — "a great cloud of witnesses" — stands in the bleachers to cheer us on to the finish line (Heb. 12:1). And we need to pray for each other.

Value Persistence

We need endurance because life is tough. Things go from bad to worse (2 Tim. 3:12-13). "We must go through many hardships to enter the kingdom of God" (Acts 14:22). Jesus Himself put it this way: "In this world you will have trouble" (John 16:33).

What I hear and observe tells me that we minister to people who feel they've accomplished a lot simply by making it through another week. Sometimes we who minister wonder how we will make it through another week.

So, let's hear it for the drab and vexing and strenuous virtue of endurance. Remember, just hanging in there can be heroic. And let's not forget that someday God will throw a party for us who persevere.

For Personal Meditation & Group Discussion

1. What kinds of things often make you want to stop trying or quit investing yourself? Do they fall into a category (criticism of you or your loved ones, unrealistic demands, unfair treatment, *almost anything* at a certain time of the month)?

2. Who's your most encouraging example of endurance and why?

3. I saw a sign that said, "It's always too soon to give up." Is that true, or it there a time to let go? How do you know when that time comes?

4. Meditate on 1 Corinthians 4:12-13 and 2 Corinthians 6:3-10. What thought do you like best in these passages? What idea do you like least in them? What does God say to you through them?

5. What keeps you persevering?

Dear friend,

Honestly, how many times have you felt like walking away from your ministry this week? This month? This year? Do you have a resignation letter somewhere in your files, all ready to date and sign? And have you wished you could turn in your mommy button any time lately? Or give your husband back to his mommy? What about moving away from a neighbor who feels it's her duty to keep the community ship-shape according to her definition? Dare we go deeper and ask if you've wanted to tell God He asks too much or gives too little?

When faced with stress, we often opt for fight or flight. I've discovered women — Christian women — (because we're so nice) are inclined to flee. We do this any number of ways. Emotional withdrawal. Leave the scene. Give up. Quit.

Three times in the last week I said to myself, I don't need this! I want out! (I won't tell you the who, what, or why involved in that sentiment.) But in my heart I place a high priority on sticking things out. I've been a Christian more than 50 years, married almost 38 years, been a mother for 31 years, and held my present job for nine. I'm in for the long haul because I take a long view. My goal is God's "well done good and faithful servant."

Using my Bible software program, I fed in words such as persevere, perseverance, endure, and endurance, limiting the range of the search to the New Testament. Wow! There are so many passages on the subject. God obviously values what Eugene Peterson translates as "passionate persistence" in *The*

Message. Maybe we, also, should give preeminence to this virtue.

I salute all you who stay the course.

Warmly,

Pamela

6
When Your Reality Check Bounces

I heard Gala Dallmann speak to women upon her return to the USA at the end of her first term of missionary service. Impressed with her candor and humility, I interviewed her for this chapter. She's got clarity that it all begins and ends with God and His grace.

Had you had missionary experience prior to going to Cameroon?

While in college I did a short-term with Campus Crusade for Christ showing the *Jesus* film for about three months in Kenya. After I was married, John and I went to Ethiopia for a year and a half with our two children. Then for the past two and a half years we were in Cameroon, West Africa.

How did you wind up being a missionary?

I received Jesus as my personal Savior when I was six. Sharing Christ was a priority in our home, but I didn't glimpse beyond the USA until I was ten and saw a film at school about Panama. I knew then I wanted to tell about the Savior to people who didn't have the chance to hear of Christ. I can't actually say I had a "call"; I just saw the great need for people to hear of Christ. I majored in Bible and nutrition to help people physically as well as spiritually.

Tell us a bit about your children.

Jonathan (8) is very focused on his specific area of interest. Right now it's sports, but he'd rather watch the game and read the stats than play. Luke (6) is sensitive to people's feelings and is my biggest helper. He's the shyest, yet craves friends. He seems to make friends everywhere we go. Josiah (4), our happy-go-lucky guy, keeps us laughing. He easily makes friends and *always* has plenty to talk about. Elissa (2) is already quite the leader, bossing her brothers around — and anyone else within hearing distance. She's friendly, outgoing, and turns the charm on or off, depending on her moods. She has lightening-quick moods! [Since this interview, Gala has become mother to a fifth child, a son named Titus.]

What are your feelings about bringing up children in Cameroon?

Living in Cameroon puts my children away from many of the negative influences in the States — like television. The pace in Cameroon is slower, so we have more family time — reading books and playing games. Cameroonians value relationships, and a healthy dose of this attitude can be good for the kids. They're exposed to different cultures, languages, and situations. They see missions firsthand and help us as we minister. I think they learn to trust the Lord, watching their parents being forced to trust in overwhelming situations.

On the negative side, they don't have the influence and input of their extended family, church, or Sunday school. They say hello and good-bye so often that they find it more difficult to establish close relationships with others. They feel out of it wherever they are. They're not Cameroonians, but don't really feel at home in America either. They're also isolated from some of their interests.

What didn't you know about serving God that you wish you'd known before going out for your first term?

When I left for the field my attitude was, "Here I come, God. I want to serve You because that will make You happy. The harder it is the better, because that should make You happier with me." That attitude took me through living in the bush in a mud hut on a Fulani compound and learning Fulfulde with three kids and expecting the fourth. That attitude held through delivering our baby at a mission hospital and then flying with seven-day-old Elissa to a remote mission station where we lived for the next year — nine hours from the nearest missionary and with limited radio contact. I wasn't forced; I chose to do this because the need of the Fulani was great, and I was pleasing God. Right?

As time went on, however, I found I couldn't do it! I couldn't love the Fulani with their different customs and constant visits at all hours of the day and night. I couldn't survive the loneliness with a new baby and no one to talk to in English. I couldn't take dealing with our various illnesses when there wasn't a doctor to call. Living with no grocery store and sporadic electricity, running water, and plumbing also took me to the edge.

I totally gave up and told God, "I'm trying so hard to serve You, but I keep failing. I just can't do it!" I'm sure God was relieved to hear that. I'd finally quit trying to do the job that only He could do.

Gala, in light of this, what were your major accomplishments during your first term? How do they compare with your expectations?

I'll answer the second question first. Before I left for the field, I planned to learn the language and culture. (Ha! Do you ever fully learn a language?) I planned to work with Fulani women — becoming close friends with some and eventually leading them to Christ. I planned to homeschool my children, make a home for my family, and support my husband in his ministry of water work and discipling Fulani men. And I expected to retain my sanity in all this.

I think I retained my sanity, but sometimes I doubt that! Elissa's birth was an unexpected accomplishment for which we are thankful, yet it made achieving other goals more difficult. I did homeschool my children and make a home in the bush. I did pray for my husband and saw him have an incredible ministry with Fulani men and in his well drilling. I tried to learn the language, but caring for Elissa and doing homeschooling in earnest made it hard to continue learning it. I even struggled to keep what I had learned since I didn't get out and use it as much.

As for having close Fulani friends, the culture was so vastly different that having a close friend felt impossible to me. My struggle with the language made even nominal friendship difficult. I felt ladies came mostly to talk with me just to hear my funny accent, to see the things we had in our home, or to ask me to give them something. Their unplanned visits usually came when I was schooling, changing diapers, nursing a baby, or preparing a meal — making conversation that much harder.

When we went to market or walked down the street, we were stared at and talked about. By evening everyone in the village knew where and what the white woman did in town that day. I stayed inside more and more, causing my language learning to decline and making it even harder to go out again. It was a downward spiral.

What lessons did you learn or insights did you gain as a result of your first term?

The lessons and insights I gained were my greatest accomplishments, and God did that, not me. I'm humbled by how much trouble God went to to teach my biggest lesson: that He really loves me.

Obviously my attitudes didn't reflect Christ when I was irritated and frustrated at the people we came to serve. Nor when I spent much time comparing myself to others. I compared myself to missionary wives in what they were doing or how long it took them to learn the language. I read missionary biographies and knew I'd never measure up. When I read the Bible, I saw only how I wasn't what I thought God wanted me to be. That was the crux of the matter — not being able to measure up to what I thought was His ideal.

I was on the coast in Cameroon for a week's getaway when the Lord really spoke to me through His Word. Romans 8 finally made sense. *God was not condemning me.* Nothing I did would stop His love or make His love any greater. Nothing I did would make me Christlike or more acceptable to Him. Jesus' blood and forgiveness make me pleasing to God, and He makes me become like Christ.

When I gave up and admitted my sin, I found God just wanted me to love Him and let Him show me how much He loved me. I didn't need to make desperate attempts to please

Him as if He were constantly weighing my work to see if it was good enough. As I saw how God loves me and I began to love Him in return, I wanted to serve Him out of love, not because it's the right thing to do.

Things didn't get better immediately, and I have a long way to go. I still have to remind myself of God's love and rest in that. What's most important to Him is our love relationship, not my service.

I pray that when I return to the field next summer, I'll continue in this spirit of admitting wrong attitudes and my inability to serve Him. I want to rest in His great love for me.

What would you say to women — missionaries, pastors' wives, staff women — just beginning in minstry?

Probably all of the above. We tend to hide our feelings from others. We tend to uphold our image by not sharing our real feelings with people lest they think us unspiritual. Even sharing honestly with others in a similar ministry is hard because of the comparisons; you want to measure up to the others around you. ("They don't struggle with these attitudes and doubts, do they?")

I'd encourage them to admit early on that they're failures — and so is everybody else doing this job. The sooner this is settled, the better. I'd tell them to share their struggles with colleagues and friends. They'd probably find, as I did, that the more they share, the more others are willing to share their struggles as well.

Then I'd say, "Rest in God's love for you, just as you are, and learn to love Him in return. Ask Him to make you ready for what He has for you each day. Let Him do His work through you, and forget trying so hard to do it for Him."

For Personal Meditation & Group Discussion

1. How does your story compare with Gala's? With what aspects of her experience do you identify?

2. How compatible with reality were your expectations about being a pastor's wife?

3. Are you obedient to James 5:16 and with whom? If you're disobedient, can you pinpoint your resistance to this command? In what ways might confession produce wholeness and holiness in you?

4. Read Romans 8:1 and 31-39. Write a paraphrase of this Scripture, making it personally yours.

5. Have you ever told God you can't do the Christian life? Meditate on some lines from Toplady's hymn, "Rock of Ages," and consider how spiritual growth is nurtured by admitting:

> Not the labor of my hands
> Can fulfill Thy law's demands;
> …Thou must save and Thou alone.
>
> Nothing in my hands I bring,
> Simply to Thy cross I cling:
> Naked, come to Thee for dress,
> Helpless look to Thee for grace…

Dear Friend,

I shared Gala Dallmann's testimony to remind us that God is more concerned about our being than our doing. It's so easy for us to act as if our service is more important to God than our love relationship with Him.

I met Gala before she, John and their first three children left for Cameroon. I remember hearing that she was in Africa and pregnant. I remember hearing that the Dallmanns were living in the bush in a mud hut with four little kids. I remember thinking, 'If I were in that situation, only You, God, could keep me from slitting my wrists!' (I have a dramatic way of expressing myself, even — or especially — to God.) So I wasn't surprised that Gala experienced stress during her first term. I was surprised that she was so open and vulnerable about it.

We in ministry tend to have a hard time obeying the command to "confess your sins to each other" (James 5:16). Maybe it's because Roman Catholicism institutionalized confession, causing us do a pendulum swing in opposition. I suspect, however, our hesitance or refusal to confess centers more in our pride. We don't want to let others know how weak, confused, wounded, ignorant, immature, sinful we really are. But in black-ink-on-white-paper, God's Word says, "Confess your sins to each other." We can obey it or not.

Linked to the command to confess to others is "and pray for each other." When confession leads to gossip, criticism, or rejection, that's wrong, whether done to or by us. Hearing another's confession, a sacred privilege and a responsibility, is to lead to prayer. I believe we'd need fewer psychotherapists if more Christians would hear confessions and respond with God's grace and truth.

Confessing to and praying for each other has a purpose: "so that you may be healed." When Gala confessed to God, His love began to heal her. I don't have to ask her to know that as she's confessed her first-term struggles to groups in the USA, her healing has continued. Every time she's witnessed to God's sufficient love, His love has become more real in her soul. Being in her audience I observed that women loved Gala for being authentic with them, and she felt it.

I'm not advocating that we become psychological exhibitionists, baring our souls indiscriminately. We need to be appropriate about what and to whom we confess. Not everybody is safe. (Read Cloud and Townsend's *Safe People* for good insights on this matter.) My experience is, however, that we don't err so much in confessing too much as in confessing too little or not at all. What do you think?

I'm committed to being a safe person. We broken people who have been graced by God tend to be safe and gracing of others.

Warmly,

Pamela

Part 2

Relating to Self: Solid at the Center

7
What's Your Worth?

*"**Self-Esteem.** One of the unique characteristics of human beings is their ability to describe and evaluate themselves. Self-esteem is the degree of positive or negative feeling that one has as a result of such assessment"* (Baker's Encyclopedia of Psychology).

Low self-esteem is a debilitating problem among women. Christian women — even women in ministry as we are — are as vulnerable to this as anybody else.

Spotting evidence of low self-esteem is easy. We see it in negative self-talk (I'm such a klutz); in a fanatical concern or careless disregard about appearance; in fear of expressing opinions or making decisions; in failure to rebuff verbal, emotional, or physical abuse; in refusal to risk to achieve what's possible; and in accepting blame for things we didn't cause. We may find poor self-esteem at the root of physical ailments as well as such psychological problems as compulsive behaviors (eating, working, controlling), perfectionism, and chronic low-grade depression.

Importance of Healthy Self-esteem

Healthy self-esteem is vital. Why? Kari Torjessen Malcolm put it well, "The obstacle of low self-esteem keeps [women] from becoming anointed channels of God's love to people."

For example, if we don't know we're loved and valuable, we have a hard time giving love. Those with low self-esteem are too self-focused to truly love. Charles Swindoll wrote,

> It is doubtful that anyone who wrestles with an unhealthy self-image can correctly and adequately give to others. Inferiority and unselfishness cannot coexist... not in the true sense as Christ describes it.... Authentic humility in no way should be confused with... lack of self-esteem (*Improving Your Serve*).

Oh, we may do lots for others, but only to placate or please them or to keep ourselves from feeling guilty.

Also, poor self-esteem can keep us from genuinely liking people we perceive as being better than we. When we don't measure up as we think we ought, seeing another achieve is like rubbing salt into the raw wound of our mutilated self-concept. A woman's letter to an advice columnist perfectly illustrates this:

> Dear Ann Landers, I have a close friend who makes me miserable. I will call her Cindy. We were pregnant at the same time. I gained 60 pounds. She gained 22. We both wanted girls so bad we could taste it. I had a boy. Cindy had a girl. I [can't get] my weight down. Cindy... is in terrific shape. I am so jealous I can't see straight.... I find it difficult to be civil to Cindy because she has beaten me at everything. I'm sure she senses my hostility because she calls me less and less.

Sometimes low self-esteem prompts us to act superior as a cover-up. Hiding behind a facade of always being right, we resent anyone challenging our opinions or questioning our judgments. We must win arguments. We dare not admit fault or apologize. We may snobbishly associate with only "the right people," as if being friends with the poor or uneducated somehow detracts from our worth. On the other hand, we may feel comfortable relating only with those we consider inferior to us because we need to feel we're better than they.

Poor self-esteem makes it difficult to receive love. Some have destroyed marriages, prompted their children's rebellion, antagonized work associates, and driven away would-be friends because they feel undeserving of happiness. Jody Foster spoke of a fellow actress to an interviewer, "The funniest part about her is she's supposed to be the prettiest girl in the world, but she thinks she's incredibly ugly, she considers herself grotesque. That's why she can't trust anyone who says they love her. It's like,... 'If you love me, you must be a real jerk.'"

What's the Source of the Problem?

Why does everyone — even a believer — find it hard to believe she has worth? I suggest two reasons.

First, our world has a distorted view of people. When God and the Bible aren't our final authority, people are devalued. A philosophy that teaches there's no omnipotent Being who created humanity leads to seeing people as mere animals, though (perhaps) with higher intelligence. In this scheme, an individual is just a tiny, dispensable cog in the big, impersonal cosmic machine.

Stuart Briscoe noted that, "If God is excluded from the Bible definition [of a person]... what is left? Man is a creature, living in a world, made somehow for something to live somewhere! What a nebulous, pointless existence this is, and yet this is the meaningless principle upon which countless lives are being lived today" (*The Fulness of Christ*). This principle leads to using people as objects that exist for one's convenience and comfort. If we've been belittled or abused by parents, harshly criticized by a spouse, disrespected by children, betrayed by friends, or rejected by church members, it's easy to assume we're drastically defective.

Second, our world has a distorted view of things. The tendency is to love things and use people, rather than love people and use things. As a result, appearance, fame, money, education, power, prestige, and how these things are obtained have been assigned unreasonable worth.

Overvaluing physical appearance has blighted the souls of us women. A women's magazine survey a few years back showed that if women could change one thing about themselves it would be their body. It reminds me of a line from the Janis Ian song, *At Seventeen:* "I learned the truth at seventeen/ That love was meant for beauty queens/And high school girls with clear-skinned smiles." Beauty may be only skin deep, but ugly goes clear to the bone.

If we toss in the matter of brains, then some of us have felt dumb since reading class in first grade or maybe freshman algebra. Nobody told us there are all kinds of intelligence that never get graded in school. Possessions? Some of us work feverishly to get the latest fashions, expensive cars, and big houses in order to buy a sense of worth.

To sum it up, if we're a poor, plain Polly with average intelligence, we probably don't get the kind of feedback that tells us we're lovable and valued. Even a gorgeous Gerty with a Ph.D.

and a Mercedes will have a hard time maintaining good self-esteem because the whole system is so slippery.

Loving Who God Loves

Yet people rightly ask, "Is respecting myself biblical? Doesn't the Bible say I'm to hate myself?"

I believe in the reality of sin, that all of us are sinners, and that we're not to hate ourselves. *We Christians are to love what God loves and hate what God hates.* God loves and values people even when He hates their sinful behavior. Likewise, you and I need to love people, including ourselves, and hate our sin. But how do we gain biblical, healthy self-esteem?

First, we must take responsibility for the way we feel about ourselves. No human gives the gift of self-worth to us. A magnet on my refrigerator reminds me of Eleanor Roosevelt's saying, "No one can make you feel inferior without your consent." And the lady had a harshly critical mother-in-law and a philandering husband! If the whole world calls you a turkey, you don't have to gobble. You can decide to believe you're an eagle. You can walk, talk, think, and act like an eagle. You can trust your security and significance in Christ.

Second, we must reject the world's value system. "Do not be conformed to this world" (Rom. 12:2). We don't have to buy the world's concept of what beauty is or what smart is or what riches are. While we make some accommodations to our culture (not dressing like the Amish, for example), we won't let the world or any person in it define our worth. We resist being squeezed into the world's mold.

Third, we accept the scriptural truth that we have worth because God says so. Say this until it sticks to the walls of your soul: "The truest thing about me is what God has said about me."

What has God said about you? The Bible says *God the Father created us in His image.* And He doesn't make junk. Each of us is God's divinely original, one-of-a-kind, valuable, deeply cherished masterpiece of a woman. And *God the Son redeemed us.* God loved us so much that He would rather die than be without our love. So Jesus lived and died and lived again to make us a part of God's family. How much are you worth? Jesus thought you are worth His very life. And *God the Holy Spirit indwells and empowers and gifts you to grow and serve.* God has chosen your body as His temple so that, in the words of A.W. Tozer, you are the dwelling place of God. He is working in us to help us to be what He wants us to be and gifted us to do what He wants us to do — all this because of His great grace.

In words and actions, then, God has given us every reason to have good self-esteem. If we cling to a sense of worthlessness, we say God has lied and we're so defective that even Jesus can't love us. That's pure, unadulterated unbelief.

The Process

Because many of us have had low self-esteem reinforced over many years, we must consciously and intentionally go through a process of reprogramming our thinking so that we think about ourselves as God thinks of us. 1) We will monitor our self-talk and stop engaging in verbal self-abuse and lies. (No more beating yourself up when you make a mistake.) 2) We will give ourselves the right to be human, imperfect, small, weak, and needy. (We don't feel worthless because we're not a good cook, have PMS, hate to clean toilets, or forget to send greeting cards on time.) 3) We will carefully weigh what others say about us both verbally and non-verbally to see if it contains God's truth. (It may not.) 4) Since our self-esteem is generally fragile and under regular assault, we will expect to pick ourselves up mentally by the scruff of the neck from time to time and deliberately choose to believe we have worth just because we do.

So work at gaining healthy self-esteem as an evidence of your confidence in God's love. As you do, you'll find new freedom to focus on God and others, rather than yourself.

For Personal Meditation & Group Discussion

1. How do you feel about yourself? What or who has influenced your sense of self-esteem? What currently is assaulting your self-esteem?

2. Write your own book of love letters from God. Write in it such verses as Jeremiah 31:3, John 3:16, Romans 5:8, and many, many more. Write a personalized description of God's love for you based on 1 Corinthians 13: "God's loves for me is patient and kind...."

3. Read your creation account in Genesis 1 and Psalm 139 and then meditate on Matthew 10:30. What does God's intimate involvement in making and knowing you tell you about your worth?

4. Meditate on the wonder of Romans 8:9 and 1 Corinthians 6:19.

Dear Friend,

My spiritual life took a giant leap forward when I began to understand that God loves me. Period. Not *if* I do right, or *when* I'm good, or *because* I measure up. He loves me when I'm good. He loves me when I'm bad. He loves me even if nobody else does. He loves me just the way I am today. He totally accepts me, fully forgives me, and deeply cherishes me. Right now.

Though He loves me much too much to let me stay the way I am, He won't love me a bit more than He does right now even after He's made some positive and radical changes in me. This gives me motivation and confidence to cooperate with His transforming me into the image of Christ. I believe reveling in God's value of me provides the best milieu for necessary growth to happen. Authors of a secular psychology textbook spoke God's truth when they wrote:

> It would seem logical that change would occur when one becomes unhappy enough with his or her present state. And if that is true, then the best way to get people to change would be to criticize and shame them into being better people. Similarly, if you want to change yourself, it would follow that you would need to feel bad enough about yourself that you would have to make a change. Part of the problem with this reasoning is that it confuses awareness with acceptance. Awareness of the need for change [in a particular behavior] is important.... Acceptance, on the other hand, refers to a more general feeling about oneself. It is related to self-esteem.... Thus, it is possible to believe

that in general you are a worthwhile, lovable, and acceptable person while also recognizing the need for some specific changes.... This... is one of the interesting paradoxes of human nature: to the extent that you feel accepted as you are, you are more able to change (*Adjustment: The Psychology of Change,* Miller, Yahne, Rhodes, p. 26).

I write about self-esteem because many of us are crippled in this area; our ministries are hindered as a result. If you're stuck in the process of believing your God-given worth, try studying (better yet getting a study group together) Robert S. McGee's *The Search for Significance.* I know you're lovable.

Warmly,

Pamela

8

Making Change

"We all experience change and the vast majority of us don't like it," wrote Isaac Asimov.

Our bodies change; we notice another gray hair, a new wrinkle, added pounds. Our feelings change — sometimes from one hour to the next. (Especially when the hormones are going bonkers.) Our circumstances change with the signing of a document. Our location changes; today we're here and tomorrow we've moved. Sometimes change is welcome; sometimes it's not.

We ministry wives know about change. The fact that it's rare for a pastor's children to complete 13 years of school in the same town proves it.

Transition = Loss

Given the fact that change is inevitable, it's helpful to understand the nature of transitions. All transitions begin with an ending and end with a beginning. Between that ending and the new beginning is a period of transition, a period always requiring adjustments.

Often the interval between an ending and the new beginning is uncomfortable, unsettling, and stressful. We resist letting go of the past and where we've been. It's familiar, and we've learned to function there. We feel uncertain about the future, and we're unsure of how well we'll deal with its new challenges. In the middle of this transition, we speak the truth when we say, "I don't know where I am." No wonder transitions are scary.

All transitions involve loss. That's obvious in the case of negative changes like death, being forced to resign, illness, amputations, and economic downturns. Even positive change, however, entails loss. A new marriage means no more dating or a new in-law. A new baby means no more uninterrupted nights of sleep or finding yourself married to a grandfather when you're not old enough to be a grandmother.

A primary loss produces secondary losses. For example, to lose a husband may mean losing a prayer partner, handyman, social escort, and more. To change cities means at least losing a community and church, not to mention hairdresser and gynecologist.

Transition, the Downside

Since transitions involve loss, we may expect to feel grief because of that loss. Our sadness may range from severe depression to a melancholy nostalgia about the "good old days." As Elizabeth Kubler-Ross discovered in her research, sadness is only one aspect of grief. Usually one also experiences shock or denial, bargaining, and anger before coming to acceptance.

When losses are tied to relationships, they result in confusion about our identity because we know who we are in relationship. A woman travels into foreign territory when she's no longer a wife, but a widow. Who is she if she's no longer a pastor's wife because her husband is no longer pastor of a church? What's her role if the children have left the nest?

When we lose something we were good at doing, we question our worth. "What value do I have now that I'm no longer teaching a Bible study? What's my purpose if I can't lead the worship team?"

Transition, the Upside

Though we hate the idea when we're in the midst of change, transitions offer opportunities for growth. Sometimes, however, it's only after we get through the transition that we can perceive any positive value in what we've been through.

Change also presents us with new choices. We can make decisions that may not have been open to us before. For example, emptying my nest presented me with the option of attending graduate school. I read a book written by a widow who mentioned her pain and the scary decisions she had to make, but she also noted enjoyable choices she was free to make — like reading in bed until 2 a.m.

Changes are usually a mixed bag of positive and negative opportunities and choices. Our ambivalent feelings and thoughts reflect this. Thus, a pastor's wife may look forward to going to a new church but feel pain at losing proximity with dear friends in the old church.

Your AQ

Some people handle change well; others have low tolerance for it. Some people are more resilient and flexible than others. A person's ability to adjust to situations may depend on the situation. In some circumstances she adjusts easily; in others, she struggles.

In any case, people who have less adaptability and elasticity in their makeup aren't necessarily lesser Christians or human beings than those who have more. As in many differences in personality and temperament, it's not a matter of good or bad or right or wrong. It's just a difference in Adaptability Quotient. Still, we can learn to handle change in healthy ways.

Strategies for Coping

Everybody who handles transitions well has learned strategies for coping. Here are some.

Cognitive strategies include naming the fear, asking the worst that can happen, breaking the problem down into smaller pieces to make dealing with it easier, ascertaining the meaning we assign to the loss. Another is to use positive, encouraging self-talk and to consider the benefits of the change. Reading books, attending seminars, and seeking wise counsel can help. Writing in a journal can clarify both the negative and positive aspects of the transition.

Emotional strategies allow us to pamper ourselves just a bit when transitioning is hitting us hardest. We take a bubble bath. Realize that chocolate has medicinal qualities. Spend a few dollars on ourselves. Read a book that doesn't improve our mind. Do something we enjoy. Make a long-distance phone call that will connect us with a Barnabas. Don't assume we have to have a stiff upper lip and go it alone. Reach out to people and be honest about our confusion or pain.

Behavioral and physical strategies encourage us to attend to our nutrition, sleep, and exercise. In the thick of the stress, we set short-term goals (today or this week); we live one day at a time. We do a small project we can easily finish in order to gain a sense of accomplishment. We set up some structure. If something big is out of control, we make a decision or take action in an area we can control.

Spiritual strategies bring our sovereign God into the equation. We choose to be totally, brutally honest with our Best Friend and Abba about how we're feeling, since He's big enough to handle the rage or despair our circumstances arouse. We read the lament and imprecatory Psalms in *The Message* and pray them as if we were writing them. We look for God's goodness in small and large ways. We listen to music that lifts our spirits. We enlist prayer support. We visualize sitting in God's lap and being comforted by Him. We heave our burden onto God's shoulders and leave it with Him until we must pick it up once more to do the work of adjusting to change. The hymn writer, Henry F. Lyte, expressed our prayer as we deal with change:

Change and decay in all around I see.
Help of the helpless, oh, abide with me!

Somebody said, "When you're through changing, you're through." Through as in dead. We're going to confront change from now until we leave time and transition into eternity, where we're face to face with the One who is the same yesterday, today, and forever.

We have a choice. We can accept this reality with as much of a positive attitude as we can muster and adapt and adjust to the changes. Or we can resist change and make life difficult for ourselves and others.

It's OK to hate a change and to mourn the loss change brings. The fact remains that making change is part and parcel of life on Planet Earth. The good news is that wherever we are at any time in our lives, God is there with and for us. If we're open to it, we usually find that some of His friends are there with and for us as well.

For Personal Meditation & Group Discussion

1. If tomorrow you were an orphan, single, childless, and/or no longer a pastor's wife, who would you be?

2. If tomorrow you became totally paralyzed, dependent on others to feed you and even brush your teeth, how would you sustain a sense of your worth?

3. What is the toughest transition you have ever made? What made that change so hard? What got you through it with your faith and sanity intact?

4. *Meditate on this:* "I the Lord do not change" (Mal. 3:6). "In the beginning you laid the foundations of the earth, and the heavens are the work of your hands. They will perish, but you remain; they will all wear out like a garment. Like clothing you will change them and they will be discarded. But you remain the same, and your years will never end" (Ps. 102:25-27). "Blessed is [s]he whose help is the God of Jacob, whose hope is in the Lord [her] God, the Maker of heaven and earth, the sea, and everything in them — the Lord, who remains faithful forever" (Ps. 146:5-6). "Jesus Christ is the same yesterday and today and forever" (Heb. 13:8). What do these words say to you about dealing with transitions?

5. What will you do to prepare yourself physically, mentally, emotionally, and spiritually for transitions into future life stages and situations?

Dear Friend,

In the year of our Lord 2000, I looked back over a decade of tremendous changes. I emptied my nest — for a while. I became a mother-in-law. I became a grandmother. I went to seminary and got a degree. I got braces on my teeth. My husband lost a job and experienced a major depressive episode. We had to sell a home I'd expected to live in until I got too old to take care of it. We adopted a child at age 56. I had to learn how to be a working mother. Any one of these changes alone can be traumatic; the accumulation of them was traumatic.

All the transitions I've been through caused deep bruises and profuse bleeding in my soul, but I survived with my faith and sanity reasonably intact. I think I used all the coping strategies noted in this chapter. Especially being honest with God, seeking prayer support, not going it alone. A coach in the process was invaluable in assuring me I wasn't crazy, stupid, or heretical, and in giving me hope that I'd make it.

Since I anticipate living a lot longer, I'm not done with making transitions. Neither are you, since you aren't dead yet.

I ask some questions about potential future changes as I look ahead: What will life feel like after I've had to bury both my parents? How will I handle retirement? How will I deal with being a widow since statistics indicate I'll outlive my husband by about seven years? What if my health declines as is normal as one ages? Yes, I have many endings and new beginnings to face in the years to come.

The transition I look forward to with eagerness is the one from here to Heaven to live eternally with my Abba Father.

Meanwhile, by His grace I intend to reframe unwanted changes and see difficult transitions not as problems, but as challenges and opportunities to gain greater clarity on who He is and to discover that He is enough for all my needs.

Warmly,

Pamela

9
Filling Up When You're Running on Empty

The following was written by a pastor's wife, who asked to remain anonymous. I think you'll find it as perceptive, honest, and encouraging as I did.

Throughout the years I've enjoyed my role as a pastor's wife. I've sensed my call is to love those in our congregation, for "love covers over a multitude of sins" (1 Pet. 4:8). I've felt the love of the people in our church and have been fulfilled and happy in my role. Over the past few years, however, I've had a sense of being overwhelmed.

Overwhelmed as Wife and Mother

We have five children, and I homeschool them. My husband

has basically been bivocational — being a pastor and in the military reserves. His military salary has enabled us to live comfortably. It also means that I've been a single parent for 45 days a year when he has done Army "stuff."

I didn't resent my husband's being gone because it decreased financial pressure; nevertheless, his absence was stressful. The tension didn't end immediately when he came home from Army duty because, though I was sick of parenting alone, he was too tired to resume parental tasks.

Overwhelmed as Pastor's Wife

Our home is right behind the church. This has been an asset mostly, but sometimes the proximity has added stress as well. For example, our church has the wonderful problem of running out of space. Our solution has been to hold two Sunday school classes in our home on Sunday mornings. While generally I'm very happy to open my home for this, it creates certain pressures.

Occasionally people have commented that our home is "church property," and you'd think our possessions in our home belong to them as well. In addition, our children have been blamed for things at church that they've had nothing to do with — just because we live so close to the church. Chalk up another stress.

Last spring and summer, three different churches contacted my husband about the possibility of having him as their pastor. I've been so happy where I am that it took me some time and prayer even to think about leaving this place.

The process of considering a call, grieving over the possibility of leaving people we love, and yet being excited about a potential move taxed my emotional system even further.

Then the Bottom Dropped Out

One day the bottom just dropped out of my life. Life became too overwhelming. I simply had no more emotional reserves to pull me through the pressures of living. I quit caring. I cried a lot. I couldn't make decisions. It was difficult taking care of the kids. I felt utterly exhausted, but couldn't sleep more than three hours a night.

Both a good friend of the family and a doctor, who happens to be a leader in our church, realized that my husband and I were struggling. The church council got together and invited us to the meeting. I felt so loved and cared for in that meeting.

A Sensitive Church Cares

During that summer, the church encouraged us to take a modified sabbatical. That meant we were to take it easy, doing as little as we could get by with while my husband still preached.

My husband resigned his Army commission, and the church voted to compensate him for the amount of salary he lost as a result.

A couple of close friends did a lot to love and encourage me through this time. I also began to take an antidepressant and entered counseling.

Learning to Fill My Tank

I've learned what caused my emotional tank to get so low. I'm discovering ways to build up my emotional reserves so that when I go off the medication I'll be able to handle the normal stresses of living and ministering.

I've come to the conclusion that I've not paid enough attention to my emotional needs. While I've been careful to tend to my spiritual needs and to keep physically fit, I didn't have a clue that I was ignoring my emotional self. I don't think

I even knew how to fill my emotional tank.

While reading *How to Beat Burnout* by Minirth, Hawkins, Meier, and Flournoy, I came across a list of things to do to start to spiral upward emotionally. I need to incorporate these things into my life more. A partial list of helpful practices is:

- Laughing.
- Practicing positive self-talk.
- Taking time for relaxation and recreation.
- Doing something good for one person each week.
- Talking with my spouse about my feelings.
- Having one positive social contact daily.

Another pastor's wife in our area is going through this very same process. It's been good for me to have someone who understands what I'm experiencing. It's helped my husband to be able to talk with her husband and compare notes. If it's true that pastors' wives are on the top of the list for emotional burnout, I wonder how many other pastors' wives have been neglecting their emotional well-being and are feeling overwhelmed, on the edge or depressed. Maybe there are many of us needing some education about caring for our emotional needs.

New Ways of Being

What I've been through has taught me a lot of new things. I've slowed down considerably. I've learned to delegate. I've learned to say no. I've worked on new friendships. And, oh yes, God showed my husband and me that He still wants us in this church — something that makes us both happy. Though I've been through a difficult year, it's been a time of experiencing the reality that God is gracious.

DETECTING BURNOUT

Made by God as both physical and emotional creatures, we can't separate these two aspects of our selves: Our feelings have an impact on our bodies, and our bodies can cause emotional upheaval.

I've observed that often women haven't stopped to feel what's going on inside them. They may be running on empty — courting serious problems — and not even be aware of it. Here's a checklist of symptoms. Do you...

- Feel generally tired and fatigued?
- Feel overwhelmingly bored?
- No longer enjoy what used to delight you?
- Feel generally sad?
- Sleep too much or too little?
- Brood over the past and how your life has turned out?
- Feel pessimistic or hopeless about the future?
- Overreact to trivial events?
- Feel irritable rather quickly and easily?
- Have trouble concentrating?
- Find that you can't remember as well as you used to?
- Eat less resulting in weight loss or overeat resulting in weight gain — a change from your normal eating habits?
- Feel disinterested in how you look so that you neglect your appearance?
- Have frequent thoughts of death and consider death as a welcomed solution to your life?

If you answer positively to many of the above questions or you feel on the edge and ready to fall over (but can't think of any reason why you should feel that way), the first step to take is to have a good physical examination. Dietary deficiency, premenstrual syndrome, menopause, and many other biological factors can create all the symptoms of burnout.

For Personal Meditation & Group Discussion

1. God's people aren't gathered in one theocratic nation; we're "scattered among all nations," with the consequences described in Deuteronomy 28:64-67. Why are those same results logical for us believers living in a fallen world?

2. Ministry couples can work hard without seeing reward for their labor. They have no guarantees that the church they build won't be torn down after they leave. Read Ecclesiastes 2:17-23 and then Galatians 6:9. How does the promise of a harvest at the proper time protect your heart from "despair over all my toilsome labor"?

3. Read John 4:6 and 8 and notice two things Jesus did to deal with His tiredness. Read Luke 5:16 for His secret to avoiding burnout.

4. According to Luke 9:10, what did Jesus do with His disciples after they returned from doing ministry? Study Exodus 20:8-11 and Mark 2:27. How do you feel about (not always the same as think about) withdrawing and resting?

5. When Nehemiah was depressed, he asked for help and got it. (See 2:1-6.) Do you let others know your needs? Why or why not?

6. Read Proverbs 17:22. Do you intentionally plan fun times for "medicinal purposes"?

Dear Friend,

I'm deeply grateful to the pastor's wife who shared her story so vulnerably. I don't believe her experience is unusual. She says she knew of only one other pastor's wife in her district who had also been hit with emotional depletion, but I'm sure there are more like her in her city, and multiplied numbers of sisters-under-the-skin across the country.

Some of us hate to admit weakness. We don't like to think that terms like burnout, depression, and despair can apply to us. Somehow, really good Christians should be above all that, shouldn't they?

We who follow Christ would get a lot further down the pike in our spiritual lives if we'd jettison ideas about what we should or shouldn't feel and deal with what is. After all, it's not as if denying our frailty and faults makes them nonexistent. So we do well to stop stonewalling by saying we "feel a little down" or we're "a bit upset" or make any other statement that minimizes the reality that we're running on empty, we're on the edge, we're depressed, or we're burned out.

We can't grow unless we're willing to be realistic about where we are. (Is this what Scripture means by not thinking more highly of ourselves than we ought to think? By having sober judgment?) At least half of the solution to a problem is defining it, and this is especially true of emotional problems.

Though I'm not often depressed, I've experienced depression. I've known "Monday Depression," my term for feeling totally depleted of my resources — physically, emotionally, mentally and spiritually — after a weekend of giving away lots of myself in a retreat ministry. Yes, I'm finite. I don't have an inexhaustible supply of energy, and its depletion has an impact on every aspect of my personality.

I've learned to recognize my tiredness, and I try to do what Jesus did: withdraw. I stop working as soon as practicably possible. I "get apart" or I'll "come apart" in ways that aren't pretty! So I sleep. Relax. Do something fun. Journal. Read. Pray.

Sometimes, however, our depletion gets ahead of us, and we burn out before we're aware of what's going on. When that happens, it's smart to seek help from medical doctors and counselors. In fact, to ignore depression can be life threatening. So take care of yourself as the valuable person you are to God.

Warmly,

Pamela

10
Mending Stress Fractures

I'm a recovering Type A mother with a Type B child. It will *always* take my daughter twice as long to complete an activity (getting dressed or picking up her toys) as I would estimate. Stress!

My dad is in the hospital for angioplasty, my mother is too frail to be alone, and I'm 1,500 miles away. Stress!

I'm up against a tough deadline for preparing a newsletter, and I get word that my boss *must* have something from me tomorrow morning — and that something requires four hours of precious time. Stress!

I'm in Connecticut attending our church conference, and I suspect it's my gall bladder that's making me so sick. Can I fulfill my responsibilities at the conference and then get back to my doctor in Colorado, or will I end up hospitalized far from home and family? Stress!

Taken one at a time, none of the above would send me over the edge. But let four or six or ten lesser or greater stressors pile up one after the other, and that's a different story. Add a couple of nights with too little sleep, and days with too many sweets, plus a miserable cold, then I'm dangling over the edge and holding on with white-knuckled fingers.

Common Causes of Stress

"Stress is an interaction between a life situation requiring readjustment and the person's ability to cope," according to Dr. Joan Borysenko. Stress is the mental, emotional, physical, and behavioral reaction we have when confronted with any unusual demand or challenge. The challenge or demand may come from within ourselves or from those on the outside. It may be real or imagined.

Stress can come in any area of our lives. We can experience relational stress with our spouse, our children, our family of origin, our friends, and the people with whom we worship or work. Any one of these relationships may present multiple stresses. For example, just one of our children may have problems with health, teachers and learning, friends, authority, and emotional overreaction that create enormous stress on a parent.

Personal stress can be rooted in health problems, a difficult pregnancy or sterility, sexual difficulties, eating disorders, feeling unattractive or inadequate, or bad habits. Significant debt and inadequate financial resources threaten well-being. Unresolved guilt, shame, pain, and grief make for constant underlying stress.

Environmental factors can be unsatisfactory living conditions, moving from the familiar to the unfamiliar, noise pollution, and traffic congestion.

Some vocational factors are not liking our job or feeling incompetent to perform it, getting passed over for a promotion, being under-challenged or underpaid, conflict with a boss or coworkers, or violations of our values or boundaries.

Yet haven't you noticed that stressors that motivate some can fracture others? Some thrive under pressure and grow stronger, the stronger the pressure they face. Others end up completely unable to function. What some see as problems, others consider opportunities. Some bend; others break. The difference between those with strong and weak coping skills is often a matter of temperament, life experiences, perspective, the number and magnitude of the stressors at a given time, and the extent to which they hook negatively into unresolved issues from the past or tap positively into spiritual resources.

It's Not All Bad

Though we most often focus on out-of-control or debilitating stress, stress in and of itself is a neutral factor in our lives. It can even be very good. One writer noted, "Stress awakens those inner resources that give lilt and zest to our everyday lives."

We can have too little stress. This leads to a general sense of boredom, mental dullness, feeling purposeless about our life, low creativity and passion, lack of significant achievement, and being tempted to sin to create some excitement. (Think of King David, moping around the palace when his buddies were off at war, succumbing to the excitement of a dalliance with Bathsheba.)

We sometimes seek the good stress of a competitive game, an ambitious goal, or a worthwhile task. When I was in college, I purposefully put off writing papers and studying for exams for as long as practical. Why? Because I found I functioned best under reasonable pressure. Stress can energize the best in us.

Distressing Stress

Stress that distresses is a different matter altogether. It can cause us to feel overwhelmed, inadequate, irritable, scared, tense, weary, and down in the dumps, or downright depressed. It can bring on forgetfulness, sleeping or eating too little or too much, unproductive activity (going fast and getting nowhere), and self-medicating.

The body responds to such stress with indigestion, tense muscles, nervous twitches, clenched jaws, grinding teeth, tiredness, excessive sweating, dizziness, weakness, and a permanent frown. Such physical responses can escalate to high blood pressure, stroke, heart attack, ulcers, and biochemical imbalances affecting emotions. Stress can lower our resistance to disease, perhaps even cancer and arthritis.

The spiritual fallout may be feeling disconnected from God and God's people. We may doubt God's wisdom, love, and power. We may question whether prayer works. We may lose joy in ministry. We may have little or no desire to pursue growth in wholeness and holiness — the spiritual disciplines are just that many more overwhelming tasks.

Type C Persons

Most of us know about Type-A persons who live overcommitted, fast-forward, gotta-get-it-done-and-now lives. We know about Type-B low-key, noncompetitive people who live with little sense of urgency and even less drive to achieve. An article I read suggested there's the Type C person who "thrives under pressure, works best in high-stress situations, suffers none of the debilitating effects of stress. Type C is confident, committed, in control... not afraid to take risks, challenges himself [herself], and knows how to control stress" (Caroline Drewes, *Colorado Springs Gazette Telegraph,* 3/5/85-D5).

Stress isn't debilitating to the Type C (read that Coping Type) person. Such a resilient person has healthy self-confidence and self-esteem. She takes care of herself, which includes the areas of nutrition, rest, exercise, fun, and relaxation. She sets healthy boundaries. She's assertive, meaning she can stand up for her beliefs and legitimate rights. She keeps things in perspective; she tends to find humor in, rather than catastophize, negative situations. She takes responsibility for her mistakes and growth. She has a strong sense of self-efficacy, believing she can solve problems and overcome hardship. She's secure enough to reach out to her support systems — family, friends, church, and health care professionals — when she needs help.

As we might expect, women most vulnerable to stress are the opposite. They have low self-confidence and poor self-esteem. They don't exercise self-care. They hold others responsible for their well-being and feel ripped off, sad, and angry if others don't solve their problems. They act as if they can't overcome hardships, set their schedules, or take charge of their lives. (Psychologists call this attitude *learned helplessness.*) Whether they tend to acquiesce to pressure exerted by others or try to control others, they have boundary issues. They see the half-full glass as half empty — or maybe even entirely empty as they magnify problems all out of proportion.

Getting Rid of Stress?

Lewis Thomas, M.D., wrote, "Stress is simply the condition of being human" (*Late Night Thoughts on Listening to Mahler's Ninth Symphony*). I believe, therefore, we can and should do what we can to become women who can cope with the stress that comes with the territory of living in a fallen world. Elsewhere I've listed some ways to deal with the symptoms of stress, but I believe in the long run the better thing is to become adept at coping, to become Type-C women.

How can we do that? Let me mention a few beginning steps:

1. Work on improving self-image, self-esteem, and self-worth. Study Robert McGee's book, *The Search for Significance*, to gain God's perspective on your identity in Christ. This will improve your theology and also your general outlook on life.

2. Learn how to set limits on others' demands. Read and apply Cloud and Townsend's *Boundaries: How to Say Yes and How to Say No to Take Control of Your Life*. I've listened to many women talk about the stresses in their lives. I frequently observe that they have direct control over and could change about half the stressors they mention. They'd deal better with the half they can't control if they didn't take responsibility for people and things over which they have no control.

3. Get rid of bitterness, resentment, and blame. Forgive those who have wronged you so they can't disturb your peace one more day. Read Smedes' *Forgive & Forget* and Allender's *Bold Love*.

4. Unlearn any sense of learned helplessness. God made you for adult responsibilities. You can learn to solve problems and make decisions. You really can do all God asks you to do because God empowers you.

5. Develop a strong support system. The whole Bible speaks to the indispensability of relationships; we need each other. God intends to meet your needs in community. Make a couple of friends you could call at 2 a.m. if you were desperate. Find a doctor you trust and enlist his help to regain and/or maintain

your health. Contact a counselor when you feel stuck. *Seeing a counselor is vital if you suffer stress due to experiencing rape, incest, or other trauma.*

6. Ask yourself in everyday stresses, "In the scope of all eternity, how important is this thing that has me in knots?" As my friend Terri VanBrunt asks, "Is this a problem or an inconvenience?"

7. Practice the spiritual discipline of not worrying about anything and praying about everything (Phil. 4:6).

STRESS-SYMPTOM BUSTERS

Cut out caffeine ♥ Resign an old job before accepting a new one ♥ Take a deep breath ♥ Take in an afternoon matinee while the kids are at school ♥ Talk to a friend ♥ Dance to praise music ♥ Write in a journal ♥ Read a story to your child ♥ Turn off the phone and spend a day with God ♥ Take a walk ♥ Say no without explanation ♥ Have lunch with somebody fun ♥ Do something nice for somebody without her knowing you did it ♥ Buy yourself a flower at the grocery store ♥ Do neck rolls and shoulder shrugs, and touch your toes when your muscles tighten up ♥ Take a bubble bath or pamper your body some other way ♥ Delegate age-appropriate tasks to your kids ♥ Post a Bible promise at your kitchen sink to remind you that God treasures you ♥ Take a class that intrigues you ♥ Cuddle a baby ♥ Pray with a friend over the phone ♥ Take a nap ♥ Count your blessings, name them one by one ♥ Say "I feel/think this" without apologizing ♥ Watch or read something just for enjoyment ♥ Give yourself permission to do any or all of the above.

For Personal Meditation & Group Discussion

1. What is causing you stress right now? Honestly, is this an inconvenience or significant problem? What symptoms are you experiencing as a result of this stress — physically, emotionally, mentally, relationally, spiritually?

2. Can you identify any others feelings (such as worry, fear, anger) behind the feeling of stress?

3. How do you generally deal with stress? If that doesn't work, what beliefs, choices, and behaviors might help?

4. Which traits of a Type C (coping) person do you need to work on with God's help?

5. Build your own stress-busting file of Scriptural promises and insights. Begin with reading and reflecting on John 14:1, 27 and 16:33; Isaiah 26:3, 32:17, and 48:17-18; and Philippians 4:6-8.

Dear Friend,

I'm blessed with a built-in stress detector located in the muscles between my shoulder blades. When they *hurt* because I'm carrying too much, I know it's time to deal with life more effectively. Another sign of feeling overwhelmed is that I get impatient over little stuff. Another is that I can't sleep as I mentally rehearse stuff. Or I sleep, but my dreams are disturbing.

One dream occurs when I have to speak or teach somewhere, and I'm not ready. The dream is that I'm at the airport frantically trying to get myself dressed and put my makeup on at the check-in counter. This doesn't happen when I feel I've got things under control.

Some stressors I can deal with fairly simply. I can climb out of bed and process distressing thoughts in my journal. I can review options and make decisions. I can ask for and take good advice. I can cast my cares on the Lord. I can make a flight reservation, and get messages written, printed, and in my briefcase. I can list what clothes to wear at the retreat. I can go over schedules with my husband and know he's ready to be the on-duty parent. I can take a day off. I can walk the dog and stop to swing on the swings at the park. I can put on my nightie right after dinner and crawl into bed with a book.

The most difficult stressors in my life, however, are often things beyond my control. I couldn't fix my husband's depression or my daughter's mental illness. I couldn't prevent my adopted daughter's neglect and abuse. I can't restore health and vitality to my aging parents. I can't undo the consequences of others' poor choices or behaviors no matter how painfully they affect me. But I can remind myself, "For this I have Jesus." I can pray and claim God's promises. For others. For myself. I can practice healthy self-care and soul-care. I can stand guard over my thoughts and attitude. I can wait patiently and expectantly for grace, truth, and time to restore equilibrium to my life.

Stress reminds me of how human I am and how desperately dependent I am on Jesus. Dependent on Jesus isn't a bad place to live. My desire is to experience stress as the theologian, Martin Marty, says he does:

> When [stress] comes, or to ward it off, I nap. I insist that, as a recipient of grace, I see no reason to fret over guilt. As one commanded not to be anxious, I try not to worry about tomorrow. Since guilt about the past and worry about the future are what keep us from sleep, I find that this usually works. I believe in this understanding of God not in order to nap, but I nap because I have this understanding of God.

I haven't arrived, but I press on! I pray you'll join me.

Warmly,

Pamela

11

Finding Time

If you're my age, you remember this. If you're younger, well, just take my word for it.

About 30 years ago, a four-day work week was the prediction for our life at the end of the 20th century. Americans, we were told, would have to learn how to spend more leisure time than had ever been known in the history of the world. We were all going to buy recreational vehicles and have long weekends of free time.

So much for secular prophecies! We Americans now work more hours per week than any other labor force in any other country of the world. Even Japan.

No wonder I keep getting asked, "Do you think women are busier today than they used to be?" The context for the query often is a conversation revolving around the fact that women opt out of attending church events and activities because of their crowded schedules.

Excuses or Reasons?

As I've consulted with leaders of women's ministries in

churches and districts, I've heard some say that tiredness and overloaded calendars are just a poor excuse for a woman's lack of commitment. If women claim to be too burdened by demands on their time to attend the monthly women's meeting, well, they're just *too* busy. Didn't women used to attend all church functions every time the doors were opened? The problem is that women today aren't as dedicated as they used to be. Shame on them!

I can see why people might believe this. After all, we live in an age of laborsaving devices. Dishwashers. Automatic washers and dryers. Telephones. E-mail and E-shopping. Microwave ovens. Fast-food restaurants and Hamburger Helper™. Planes and trains and automobiles. And we women need every such labor- and timesaving device we can get because, despite them, we're generally busier than Grandma was.

The reality is that most of us women work outside the home and not necessarily because we're greedy and materialistic. We work to keep our daughters and sons in Christian schools and put them through college. We work to meet the mortgage on a modest home and to pay rising medical and dental costs. As ministry women, you and I work to make a difference in our world for Jesus' sake because God called us to do so.

Throw in a mother's desire to help her children develop their abilities through music, art, and sports (translate that soccer games, piano lessons, and Brownie Scouts — meaning mom as chauffeur). Add a generous handful of effort to maintain a good marriage (and we with the church's prodding expect more of our marriages than did our foremothers). Stir in a concern to be good stewards of the temple of our body, meaning a solid exercise program. Combine with school programs and parent-teacher conferences. Oh, yes, mix in time alone with God and going to church as primary ingredients. This is the recipe for many, maybe even most, women today.

Are women today busier than women used to be? Huh-*lo*-oh! Did you just drop in from outer space? Of course we're busier. I'm busier than I used to be. Aren't you?

Now we can lament such busyness until the cows come home, to use a Pennsylvania Dutch expression, but it won't change things. The more practical solution is to consider how to do more with less time. In that vein, let's talk time management. We all have 24 hours in each day. How can we make the most of them?

Laying the Foundation

Regardless of the demands made on us, we alone are responsible for the use of our time. Since we're accountable to God, we need a clear sense of His purpose for our lives so we know how we're to spend our minutes and days. (If you need help defining this, I highly recommend that you read and work through the little book, *The On-Purpose Person* by Kevin McCarthy.)

Once we define our purpose, we understand how better to set goals to fulfill our purpose and then how to order our priorities accordingly. Purpose and priorities inform us when to say yes to those things that fulfill our purpose and to say no to those that don't.

We Christians must put caring for our own souls at the top of our priority list. Soul-care is something nobody else can do for us; we can't delegate it. If we don't function well in the spiritual area, we probably won't function up to our potential in any other area of our lives — physical, emotional, intellectual, relational, or vocational.

Factored alongside our life purpose is an accurate assessment of our gifts, abilities, temperament, and energy level. We must know how God made us. Vonnette Bright used to remind women, "If God created you as a one-ring circus person, don't try to run a three-ring circus. If you can run three rings, don't settle for running one." Since God put each of us women together uniquely, He only holds us responsible to be the best we can be without comparison to another's best — or worst.

Practical Hints

Once we lay the foundation of who we are in Christ and what He's called us to be and do, we fill in our calendars, day by day, with thoughtful regard to our purpose, priorities, gifts, and energy. Still, we do well to act practically and consider how to work smarter rather than harder. Here are some suggestions culled from many sources.

Organize space: Clutter is time-consuming; therefore, unclutter your space.

- Refuse to be a packrat. Less really is more. Toss stuff you haven't use in the last two years. ("Yes, but as soon as I toss it....") Don't debate this. Do it!
- Reduce the number of knickknacks, whatnots, and brick-a-brack. If you don't absolutely cherish and value any dust-collector, it needs to go. I don't care who gave it to you, you have my permission to trash it.
- Recycle gifts you don't want or need. If you're considering renting storage space for all the banquet centerpieces you've been given for your dining table over the past decade, think Good Will. Yes, you do too have the right to decorate your home according to your taste.
- Make a place for everything and keep everything in its place. Not having to hunt for what you need saves time.

If you can't put stuff where it belongs as you go throughout your day, take 10 minutes a day to tidy things up. What 10-minute block is best for that?
- Keep a bag in your closet. Put anything in it that doesn't fit, doesn't feel right on you, or hasn't been worn in two years. Call the Salvation Army truck when you have a full bag.
- Buy a file box and file really important papers.
- Put questionably important papers in a box. If after a year you haven't reached into that box for those saved letters, articles, school notices, or whatever you toss in it, what you've got is a box of waste paper. Take it to the dumpster.
- Buy a paper accordion file for clipped recipes, using a different section for different categories of foods. On the other hand, what are the chances that you'll try that interesting recipe? Not very likely? Then don't waste space filing it.
- Rubber cement frequently used recipes to the inside of a cupboard door for easy reference.
- Ask the most organized woman you know to tell you how she does it. Ask her to walk with you through your kitchen, your office or desk, and your closets and give timesaving suggestions.

Use time twice: We women are known for multitasking. We can do two things at once. For example:
- Keep a box of cards, stationery, and stamps in your car to catch up with correspondence while you're waiting to pick kids up at school or church.
- Take the periodicals you've collected to read in the doctor's waiting room.

- Pray while you walk, bike, or drive.
- Keep a one-a-day thought or Bible verse near your sink and meditate on it while preparing a meal.
- Listen to books on tape as you do mindless tasks.
- Listen to, don't watch, CNN to catch up on the news while you're dusting or cooking.
- Clean the mirror, sink, and toilet when watching a preschooler who's playing in the bathtub.

Delegate: Since you're not superwoman, don't try to do everything that needs to be done at home, in the church, or on the job.

- Agree with your husband on what family chores you each will do.
- Assign your children age-appropriate household chores: making beds, packing lunches, dusting, emptying the dishwasher, and cleaning up after themselves. We mortgage our kids' future when we do for them what they can do for themselves — and their future spouses will hate us for it.
- Lower your standards about how good good enough is and how clean clean enough is. If you're a perfectionist, get over it.
- Ask for help when you need it. It's sometimes more blessed for you to receive than give, and you bless the giver in the process.

Plan ahead: We can waste a lot of time because we don't plan ahead.

- Create a message center near each phone — pencil and paper or small whiteboard and markers.
- Keep a running to-do list or two — one for today and one

for projects that aren't time-sensitive.
- See how many errands you can take care of on one trip around town.
- Lay out the next day's clothes the night before to save confusion in the morning.
- Get good directions to any appointment. Write them down on a sticky note and fasten it in your schedule book. Then move the note to your dashboard so you can glance at it without taking your eyes off the steering wheel.
- Have a couple emergency menus on hand at all times. Stock foods for simple meals you can fix quickly when guests drop in unexpectedly.
- Plan for leftovers to make quick meals. Cook a double recipe of foods that freeze well — one for today and one for another day when you don't have time to cook.
- Keep a box of small gifts (books, notecards, candles) for when you need a last minute gift for somebody.
- Buy birthday cards and address and stamp the envelopes for the whole year (while watching a must-see television program). File the cards by month so they'll be ready to mail.

Miscellaneous tips:
- Quickly clean with a feather duster and an electric broom when a serious housecleaning is beyond your energy or time.
- Buy time for yourself by buying a machine, appliance, or electronic marvel.
- Treat a phone as your servant; you are not its slave. You don't *have* to answer it.
- Make friends with a computer. Use computer-generated

address labels for Christmas cards, regardless of what Emily Post says. If your friends care about how the envelope is addressed, take the time you've saved to help them get a life.
- Buy from catalogs.
- For travel ease, keep a bag of toiletries packed ready for the suitcase. Put almost used-up make-up (lipstick, eyebrow pencil, and foundation) into a bag so it's ready to pack. Build your whole travel wardrobe around one neutral color — black, beige, or navy — to lighten your load and allow good mix-and-match possibilities.
- Convince yourself a good meal is tasty, nutritious, and *quick*. You don't get points for time spent in meal preparation.
- Don't try to be Martha Stewart unless you also have 400 employees.

Even if *you* get all organized so that you have time to do all God really intends for you to do, you can count on the fact that lots of people you deal with don't. Graciously challenge their priorities, if you wish. At the same time, extend them grace, remembering your church programs and events compete with endless other things for time people have too little of, money they have too little of, and energy they have too little of. This means women will stay away from church in droves if what's offered isn't worthwhile as *they* perceive worthwhile. Enough said!

And that's the way it is at the beginning of this schedule-jammed decade and century.

For Personal Meditation & Group Discussion

1. "Clocks are corrected by astronomy! What good is a clock unless it is set by the stars? Without a sense of eternity you don't even know what time it is" (R. Eugene Sterner). What are your eternal priorities that help you know what time it is? Read Esther 4:12-14 and meditate on Mordecai's words about her place in time.

2. "Great men [and women] never complain about the lack of time. Alexander the Great and John Wesley accomplished everything they did in twenty-four-hour days" (Fred Smith). What do you think is the primary difference between how different people spend the same 24 hours? Remember the psalmist's prayer, "Oh! Teach us to live well! Teach us to live wisely and well!" (90:12).

3. "When anyone asks you to give your time, they're really asking for a chunk of your life" (Antoinette Bosco). Another wrote, "What I do today is important because I'm exchanging a day of my life for it." And another, "Time is the coin of your life. Don't let anybody else spend it for you." What do these quotes tell you about others' demands on your time? On your demands for another's time?

4. "Though I am always in haste, I am never in a hurry; because I never undertake any more work than I can go through with perfect calmness of spirit" (John Wesley). Reflect on that and on Ecclesiastes 3:1-8.

5. Consider the promises of 2 Corinthians 9:8 and Galatians 6:9. How does this apply when you feel overwhelmed by demands?

Dear Friend,

Growing up in a tiny rural town five decades ago, I was in a family of five children living in a big old house with four floors, if you count a basement and finished attic with no heat. We planted a huge garden and preserved prodigious amounts of food each summer and fall. Every kid was a dishwasher. We helped Mama do laundry with a wringer washer and lugged baskets of wet clothes outside to the clothesline or on rainy days up three flights of stairs to the ropes strung in the attic. Disposable diapers? Not invented yet. Permanent press? Ditto. Ironing dresses for four little girls, each wearing seven dresses a week, made for a considerable amount of ironing. And Mama sewed almost all our clothes. We went to Sunday school, church, youth fellowship, and evening service every Sunday, plus prayer meeting on Wednesday evenings — and to revival services and missionary conventions that took up at least three weeks of every year.

Yet I remember Mama coffee-klatching with two nearby aunts while we kids played outdoors. (Mama didn't work outside the home.) Since it took most of a day and at least three families of relatives to boil up a big copper kettle of apple butter outdoors over an open fire, it was as much a social event as a task. With no television, evenings meant eating a dishpan full of popcorn while Mama read books to us or, later, eating popcorn while we adolescents did homework with three to five cousins sitting around our kitchen table. There were picnics, swimming in the river, and dads and kids playing baseball. I don't recall life feeling fast-paced or frantic. It was *Mayberry*

RFD.

Sounds like the good ol' days, doesn't it? And if we could all transport ourselves back about 50 years, wouldn't life be grand?

As a woman who finds she's used very ounce of energy she possesses at the end of almost every day, I confess I don't want to live in Hesston circa 1950. I want my dishwasher and automatic washer and dryer. I think the Nobel Prize for science belongs to the people who gave us wrinkle-free fabric. I was grateful for disposable diapers when my little girl was a baby. Truth is, I've even found store-bought apple butter to rival anything cooked up at home when I was a kid. And I don't want to make my own clothes. Been there, done that, made people feel sorry for me!

Furthermore, most of my busyness is good busyness. Even in those times when I'm weary from too much doing, I'm glad to be alive for such a time as this, despite its drain on time and energy. I like serving Jesus in ways the women I knew back in the good ol' days wouldn't have imagined. I like e-mailing a missionary half a world away to encourage her the same day I learn of a stress in her life. I like being able to fly across the country to train women to be and do all God created and called them to be and do — and then get back home before my family begins to miss me. I like all the opportunities for spiritual and professional learning and growth that abound today. I like the challenge of making my life count for God's kingdom as fully as I can.

Yes, I'm busy. So I must lean hard on God for strength to persevere, for wisdom about priorities, for God-honoring motivations, for courage to rest when I need it. I suspect you have to do this also.

Warmly,

Pamela

12

Life's Second Half

In the words of a postmenopausal comedienne, "Can we talk?" About women at midlife?

Women who have gone through "the change" number in the tens of millions. Kind of amazing, when you know the facts. Back in Jesus' day, when life expectancy for women was less than 30 years old, there weren't many who lived long enough to experience old age. At the turn of the 20th century, even, life expectancy had only inched up to 50 years old. That means that given large families, women bore children, nursed infants, cared for offspring, and died almost as soon as they had emptied their nests. Most didn't reach age 51, the average age of menopause for women since the 6th century A.D.

The Facts, Ma'am

First, let's define menopause. Technically, it's a woman's last menstrual period. A woman can figure she'd had her last period if she's not had one for a whole year. Climacteric refers to the whole time span of a woman during the termination of her ability to reproduce. Not being technical, I'll be using the word menopause in discussing this span of time before, during, and after the last period.

Sometime around age 35 a woman's ovarian function begins to fluctuate. The level of hormones produced by the ovaries, estrogen and progesterone, begins to vary. As a woman's levels of estrogen and progesterone change, her body begins to change.

Freda Kronenberg of Columbia University Hospital of Physicians and Surgeons noted, "Estrogen affects our hearts, our minds, our bones, our behavior, and our sexual function and desire." C. Sue Furman wrote, "Scientists have found that estrogen does more than spur the reproductive organs through childbearing years; it influences at least 300 body functions" (p. 15). So much for the myth that symptoms connected with menopause are all in a woman's head.

About one in ten women breeze through the change from procreative to postprocreative years without some discomfort. Since estrogen is stored in fat cells, heavier women sometimes experience fewer symptoms. (Before using that as an excuse to pack on pounds, remember the correlation between weight and heart disease, the number one killer of postmenopausal women.) At the other end of the spectrum, some women suffer many and severe symptoms, even requiring hospitalization. The majority experience something between these two extremes. The length of time a woman deals with symptoms may be two, five, or even more years.

First, the Bad News

Often the first clue of the onset of menopause is hot flashes or flushes (daytime incidents) or night sweats (nighttime occurrences). These all refer to the same experience that your thermostat has broken and the furnace is running on high. You join the "fan club" — fanning yourself with the church bulletin or the restaurant menu with one hand while mopping perspiration from your face with the other.

A woman's monthly periods begin to change. Change may mean more frequent, less frequent, heavier, or lighter.

But the laundry list of symptoms include mood swings, vaginal dryness and discomfort, insomnia, heart palpitations, malaise/depression, incontinence, short-term memory loss, crawly or tingly skin, fatigue, bone loss, difficulty concentrating, headaches, loss of libido, bloating, and more. (Makes you glad you're a woman, eh?!)

Sometimes one symptom may cause others. For example, night sweats can interrupt a woman's sleep frequently so that she becomes sleep deprived. This can result in memory lapses, headaches, irritability, and fatigue — such as we experienced when spending a night caring for a sick baby or staying up late to see our teenager meet curfew.

We might consider climacteric as adolescence in reverse. Remember how weird your body felt and how wildly your emotions bounced with puberty? Folks spoke of your raging hormones. Well, your hormones eventually got regulated and your body adjusted to the change. As hormones cease raging at menopause, once again the body must adjust to its new chemistry, and you may find yourself laughing one minute and crying the next hour — just like a teenager.

Again, menopause is not in your imagination. You're not crazy. You're not carnal, either, so don't expect to pray, confess, or claim your way to victory over problems created by decreased hormones — unless you'd treat diabetes that way also.

Lifestage Complications

But decreasing estrogen isn't the only tension a woman faces in midlife. If she's not worked outside the home before, kids' college expenses may mean making her way into the workplace. Or she finds her children leaving home and mourns the hole in the family circle. Her parents' ability to care for themselves may be declining, requiring lots of her attention. Women in midlife can get caught between the competing demands of two generations.

Just as she's trying to work through her own midlife difficulties, a woman's husband may hit a midlife crisis. He may be grieving that his youthful vision of his future isn't going to materialize. He may spiral into depression because he'll never achieve the position or money he had anticipated at age 25. Or maybe he fulfilled his dreams; he's got the temporal rewards that come with workaholism; but he questions if it all was worth what he sacrificed to attain it.

What some midlife men find they've missed out on is significant involvement in family life. In short, they want to spend more time in the nest. This can happen at the precise time when their wives, having nurtured chicks for several years, want to get out of the nest and use education and abilities they put on hold with the arrival of the first child.

A man's body, like his wife's, ages. His tummy bulges and his hairline recedes. He gets winded faster, and his legs can't get to the tennis ball or around the softball diamond with the speed they once had. Furthermore, this man finds himself married to a *grandmother* — a perhaps unwelcome reminder of his own aging process. And just as he starts feeling uneasy about the affects of age on his virility, he may find his wife compounds his doubts by postponing sexual relations because vaginal changes make that painful for her.

Perhaps the soul connection between the couple is strained also. As they gave much attention to childrearing, they failed to give attention to their marriage. One day they sat down alone at the table and found they didn't have much to say to each other.

Now, the Good News

Women face many defining events in their lives: first period, first love, first job, marriage and first home, first baby. Menopause is simply one more significant defining event in a woman's life. It ushers her into what Gail Sheehy calls the period of "Second Adulthood." She wrote, "If forty-five is the old age of youth, fifty is the youth of this Second Adulthood. In fact, we have roughly the same number of years to look forward to as we have already lived as reproductive women" (p. 41).

About 35 years span the first period and the beginning of menopausal symptoms. Given longer life expectancy, a woman may live 35 or more years after her last period. Those can be 35 *good* years. Today, a woman healthy at 52 will probably live to age 92, says Furman. "To put it in perspective, many women who celebrate their 55th birthday in 1995 [the year her book was written] will be blowing out 100 candles in the year 2050!" (p. 40).

Unlike how it was for our grandmothers, menopause doesn't need to equal a debilitating old age. While our grandmothers suffered menopause in silence and without any help in relieving its symptoms and preventing physical decline, today's women can find help. For one thing, we can talk about it with friends and realize we're not alone. Our cities may have a menopause support group. If not, we can start one. Good exercise, good nutrition with calcium and other supplements, and good rest can keep our bones strong and our skeletal and internal muscles toned — something even young women should do well before the first sign of menopause.

Also, hormone replacement therapy (HRT) can relieve many of the most annoying symptoms of menopause. It also decreases a woman's risk of heart attack, stroke, and osteoporosis (bone loss). HRT is administered by pills, patches, and shots. Hormones can be prescribed, or herbal compounds can be found in health food stores. Not every woman, however, should or wants to go on HRT. Some women worry about the risk of cancer, and that's valid when there's a family history of estrogen-fed cancer. At the same time, women are twice as likely to die of heart disease, the number one killer of women, than they are of cancer. The point is, this is a matter a woman must discuss with her doctor.

(Caution, some physicians blow off women's complaints: "What do you expect. You're getting older." If your doctor doesn't treat you with dignity, or if you suspect he/she is not up to date on the latest research (what precious little of it there is of it — menopause has not been a research priority), look for another doctor. Keep looking until you find one who doesn't want to put you on a tranquilizer or send you to a shrink. If you hear you're too young to be going through menopause, ask what your hormone levels are. *They*, not age, determine whether or not you're menopausal.)

Time to Take Stock

Midlife provides women with a wonderful opportunity to assess their lives. Who have they discovered themselves to be? What are their strengths and weaknesses? What kinds of things give them energy? What have they achieved? What skills have they learned? With what disappointments and losses must they make peace? What dreams are yet unfulfilled?

When I was 47, I realized that my grandmother had lived to age 94. Twice 47 equals 94; perhaps I had as long to live as I'd lived. I considered what I wanted to do with the second half of my life. The result was having six teeth pulled and getting orthodontic braces. Two years later I was able to chew well for the first time in my life. I also enrolled in seminary. By the time I hit 50, I had a master's degree in counseling. As graduation approached, I became national director of women's ministries for a denomination. I calculate that, in addition to being wife and mommy, this was my fourth career change, and it happened on the shady side of midlife.

Since God never thought up the idea of retirement, I believe every Christian woman can hope that the best work of her life may be in her second adulthood. Moses lived 80 years before he was prepared to answer God's call to free the Israelites from slavery — the magnum opus of his life. Our best legacy may be the service we render to God and others in our 60s or even 80s. We can ask God that we "will still bear fruit in old age." We may even hope that we'll "stay fresh and green" in our willingness to risk and grow and minister (Ps. 92:14).

Time to Affirm Godly Values

We dare not allow the world to squeeze us into its youth-adoring mold. Therefore . . .

We older women accept long life as God's blessing. Have you noticed throughout Scripture that old age was taken as proof of God's blessing? Deuteronomy 6:2 connected keeping God's decrees with enjoying long life. Proverbs 16:31 says, "Gray hair is a crown of splendor; it is attained by a righteous life." Ungodly people can live to a ripe old age, but that doesn't diminish the fact that those of us clothed in Christ's righteousness are to rejoice in old age as a gift of God.

We older women can claim God's provision for all of the days He allots us. God's promise is: "Even to your old age and gray hairs I am he, I am he who will sustain you. I have made you and I will carry you; I will sustain you and I will rescue you (Isa. 46:4).

We older women can continue to grow in grace and truth. The famous Titus 2 passage, that talks about older women teaching younger women, first instructs Titus to teach older women. "Teach the older women to be reverent in the way they live, not to be slanderers or addicted to much wine" (2:3). Even senior saints can overcome bad habits. The old song says, "The longer I serve Him the sweeter He grows." The longer we serve Jesus, the sweeter we should grow.

We older women can witness to God's goodness and faithfulness over the long haul. With the Psalmist we can say, "I was young and now I am old, yet I have never seen the righteous forsaken" (37:25). Our prayer is, "Since my youth, O God, you have taught me, and to this day I declare your marvelous deeds. Even when I am old and gray, do not forsake me, O God, till I declare your power to the next generation, your might to all who are to come" (Ps. 71:17-18). Younger generations need to hear us recount God's faithfulness to boost their own trust in Him.

We older women can affirm that true beauty is a matter of spiritual maturity. Despite the fact that our culture is obsessed with youthful beauty, we godly women "of a certain age" must intentionally internalize God's standard of attractiveness: "Charm is deceptive, and beauty is fleeting; but a woman who fears the Lord is to be praised" (Prov. 31:30).

Research done by Dr. John Williams and reported by Furman revealed that Amish women make the transition to post-reproductive years with less difficulty and even with humor. He also found that the same transition was more troublesome to women concerned with physical appearance and negative attitudes about old age (p. 41). Let's reject our cultural norms and believe God's Word:

> Your beauty should not come from outward adornment, such as braided hair and the wearing of gold jewelry and fine clothes [or a firm body and smooth skin]. Instead, it should be that of your inner self, the unfading beauty of a gentle and quiet spirit, which is of great worth in God's sight (1 Pet. 3:3-4-addition mine).

Younger women can't begin too soon to prepare for old age. All of us need to remember, as my friend Marilyn Moravec says, that life on earth is not the main event. Aging is inevitable, but how we age is not. We need, therefore, to remember our Creator in the days of our youth (Eccl. 12:1). We need also to pray with the psalmist, "Teach us to number our days aright, that we may gain a heart of wisdom" (Ps. 90:12).

Resources:

Sally Conway, *Menopause: Help and Hope for This Passage* (Grand Rapids: Zondervan Publishing House, 1990).

C. Sue Furman, *Turning Point: The Myths and Realities of Menopause* (NY: Oxford University Press, 1995).

Lois Mowday Rabey, *Coming of Age: Personal Insights on Menopause* (Nashville: Thomas Nelson Publishers, 1995).

Gail Sheehy, *The Silent Passage* (New York: Random House, 1992).

For Personal Meditation & Group Discussion

1. What were the messages you received about menopause from your mother or grandmother? What are your feelings about menopause?

2. What insights does this newsletter give you about yourself or your female relatives, friends, and colleagues in work and ministry regarding midlife issues? Does what you've read explain the behaviors and moods of any of these women?

3. How many women in your church are in their 40s and 50s? Has your church offered a program for helping them deal with midlife issues? If not, what might be the advantages of doing so?

4. Are there older women you admire and wish to emulate? Who are they? What characterizes their lives? Do a study focusing on the older women of the Bible and note positive traits you'd like to develop or negative ones you'd like to resist.

5. Meditate on Psalm 92:12-15 and write your thoughts in your journal:

> The righteous will flourish like a palm tree,
> ...planted in the house of the Lord,
>   they will flourish in the courts of our God.
> They will still bear fruit in old age,
>   they will stay fresh and green,
> proclaiming, "The Lord is upright;
>   he is my Rock, and there is no wickedness in him."

Dear Friend,

I'm a little slow, but not stupid. I often ask women in ministry, "What issues do you feel you need help with?" Over a period of about four years I've had one woman and then another and another answer, "Women at midlife." Finally, this keen mind of mine had a flash of insight: many women wanted more information on the issue of women facing menopause.

If you're in your 40s and 50s, you already know that this subject is important.

If you're in your 20s and 30s, you may think you don't need to think about menopause yet — and you couldn't be more wrong. Some women — very few — have premature menopause in their 20s and 30s. Since ovarian function begins to fluctuate in most women around age 35, before age 40 all women do well to take steps to ensure good health in their old age.

If you're over 60, you may be wondering what a nice Christian woman is doing talking about something so *personal* and *private*. But as I once heard Howard Hendricks of Dallas Seminary say, "I'm not ashamed to discuss what God was not ashamed to create."

At almost 58, I'm what the books call "postmenopausal." I know what I have experienced getting to where I am now, but I had no way of knowing whether my experience was typical or not. My mother never mentioned her menopause to me, and we could talk about almost anything. Since I wasn't living at home at the time, I didn't see the affects of it on her. I never read a book on the subject until I researched this chapter. I did go to my physician complaining of some symptoms a few years ago. For one, I told him I often felt like I was on a caffeine jag even though I avoided caffeine like poison. My doctor examined me and said, "Yep, you're in the rip-roaring middle of menopause." He told me what to do about it, and I did what he recommended without questioning.

In the last couple of weeks I've educated myself. I collected material from the Internet and read several books on the subject. I've discovered some symptoms I hadn't mentioned to my gynecologist are all a part of the package. I've included a list of some of the materials I've read in case you may want to check them out for yourselves.

I find I'm looking at women with new understanding as a result of my research. I think, Whew! Most of the women I work with in leadership are at this crucial stage in their lives. They're experiencing the stresses of major physical changes and problematic symptoms. They're perhaps dealing with the emotional upheaval caused by body chemistry going bonkers. I need to understand this as I relate to them. I think I've expanded my capacity for insight and empathy as a result of immersing myself in the subject of menopause.

I pray the facts of this chapter will help you understand yourself and other women better. I trust it will enable you to reach out to others, either to give or receive help and support.

Warmly,

Pamela

Part 3

Relating to Family: An Example of Truth & Grace

13
When Criticism about Him Hurts You

The old saying, "Sticks and stones may break my bones, but words will never hurt me," is a patent falsehood. We know that verbal abuse can be as painful as physical abuse. Bruises on a body sometimes heal more quickly than assaults on a soul.

Perhaps that's why a survey I took of pastors' wives revealed that dealing with criticism is a major issue. Criticism of her husband can indeed be one of the most painful situations a pastor's wife confronts. Four ministry wives graciously shared their insights. I think the principles apply to all women in leadership in the church. So listen in to my conversation with Nancy, Jackie, Cynthia, and Vicki.

PHH: Why is criticism about a husband such an issue for a pastor's wife?

Nancy: I suppose it becomes an issue because many times our husband's ministry is at stake. Criticism can force a family to move from a church, home, and schools they love.

Vicki: Yes, we have to deal with such questions as: What will happen to us if we are asked to leave? Will we find another church? Will we be strong enough emotionally to begin again? Will my husband be devastated by this and leave the ministry? What about our reputation?

Cynthia: I believe that when a wife sees her husband suffer, it is hard for her not to make a big issue about unjust — or even just — criticism.

Vicki: That's true. When you criticize my husband, you are criticizing a part of me. The pastorate is a profession where goals, visions, burdens, and responsibilities are intimately shared. His job is my job as well, so we share feelings of failure. Also, because we make ourselves open, honest, available, and vulnerable to our church family, criticism feels like rejection of our inner selves.

Jackie: On top of this, a pastor is his wife's pastor as well as her husband, and she must esteem him in his role as pastor. Criticism can undermine a wife's respect for her pastor-husband.

Vicki: An added problem is that a pastor's wife can't confide in anybody within the congregation in these situations. This can result in mistrust of closest friends, of one's self, and even of one's calling.

PHH: Do you think pastors come in for more criticism than other people do? Is a congregation more likely to criticize a pastor than they are the organist or head deacon?

Jackie: It's human nature to criticize authority figures. That plus the fact that people hold them up in unreal loftiness means they come in for more criticism.

Cynthia: And people tend to evaluate a pastor based on the success of the church.

Vicki: I think American congregations feel much competition with other churches and between denominations. If your church is not moving fast enough (or if it's moving too fast for some people's comfort), the pastor is an easy target for blame.

Nancy: Pastors come in for more criticism because in most churches the pastor is the head, and people eventually answer to him. So why not aim directly at the "top man"? Maybe this saves time!

Vicki: I think pastors often are not honest about their humanness. Deep down, people want their pastors to be "superhuman" and many pastors fall into the trap of portraying that image — and eventually fail.

Jackie: If a pastor loves his people and is vulnerable with them, I feel people aren't quite as critical with him. If the pastor is critical, then he can expect criticism back.

PHH: When your husband is being criticized, do you usually hear it directly or indirectly through another?

Cynthia: I hear it both ways, depending on the kind of person. I hear from fearful or nonconfrontive people through others.

Jackie: I usually hear criticism indirectly. A third party brings it to my attention.

Nancy: Most often I hear it directly.

PHH: What do you think prompts people to report to you the negative comments about your husband that others have made?

Jackie: Some people are afraid to speak their minds to the pastor and want others to run interference for them. The problem with this is that the criticizer may just have been venting and never intended it to get to the pastor.

Nancy: Some people may genuinely think this will help. Maybe they want me to warn my husband about problems.

Cynthia: Some are truly committed to us and out of love want to share what others are saying. That's not the majority. Some are just bitter or unhappy with their own lives.

PHH: How do you handle it when people criticize your husband to you directly?

Nancy: I say sincerely and kindly: "I appreciate your sincerity and honesty in coming to me. You have said it so clearly and directly. I'm sure my husband would rather hear this from you than me. Here's where you can reach him." Most don't follow through. Those who do can be talked and prayed with and the problem worked out.

Cynthia: If I believe the person is committed to us and to walking with the Lord, I'm open to them. Usually I send them to my husband directly, and that usually puts an end to it.

Vicki: I do not feel a need to defend my husband, and I do not engage in negative conversation pertaining to him. If the criticism is not of a serious nature I may chuckle and say, "Yes, I know he's sometimes that way, but he's working on it!" If it's more serious, I tell the person that maybe he or she should talk to him about it. Then I change the subject.

Jackie: I try to be sensitive to the persons and evaluate what they're saying. I usually try to help the criticizers see the situation from my husband's or Scripture's perspective. Then I pray with them about the issue. If necessary, I take it to my husband.

PHH: How do you deal with criticism you hear indirectly?

Nancy: I ignore it.

Jackie: I ignore it if it's not justified; otherwise, I talk with my husband about it.

Cynthia: It depends on the person; however, I usually request that they complain to him directly.

PHH: What are some things you've done to deal with criticism that haven't worked? Why do you think they haven't worked?

Jackie: When I came against criticism harshly, it made people defensive. When I've been hurt and severed relationships, that didn't deal with the problem.

Cynthia: I used to try to justify my husband's actions. According to Matthew 5:23-24 and 18:15-20, I now think this is unbiblical.

Nancy: I've gone to two extremes: saying nothing and blasting back. Holding back created unnecessary stress in me, and fighting back only led to further problems.

Vicki: It has not helped for me to dwell on the criticism and the character of the criticizer. That takes my focus off my Source of grace and puts me in the frame of mind of a judge.

PHH: Do you tell your husband the negative stuff you hear about him?

Cynthia: Most of the time I don't. Sometimes, however, I do when it will help him in his ministry or the way he responds to others.

Nancy: I only tell him if I've heard the criticism directly.

Vicki: I tell him only when the criticism is true and is weakening his ministry.

Jackie: That depends on my evaluation of the criticism and whom it's coming from. Telling him is sometimes important so that there isn't an undercurrent of dissension. My husband needs to bring the criticizer to account and stop any undermining of his ministry.

PHH: Assuming you're not married to a perfect man, what do you do when you know that his faults are weakening his ministry?

Vicki: The Lord showed me a few years ago that I am not to be the Holy Spirit in my husband's life. When I am, I get in the way of His fully working in his life. I am his cheerleader, and I pray about his weak areas.

Jackie: I talk about this with my husband. This isn't easy and must be done in love. We pray about it together, and he seeks the Lord.

Cynthia: First I pray for him. Over a period of time I share what I feel are the most critical areas and do whatever I can to empower him to be all that God want's him to be in that area.

Nancy: I think a lot. I pray a lot. I confront lovingly. Usually he's not aware of the problem and appreciates my input.

PHH: What's the best advice you can give about dealing with criticism about your husband?

Nancy: Jesus *never* defended His actions, and neither should we. Jesus was always on the offensive — moving and changing those around Him. Don and I have learned to let our actions, words, and lifestyle speak for themselves. We have learned with the Lord's help to love, forgive, and go the extra mile for critical people. People can be changed and churches revitalized, but there's always pain in the process. Criticism is painful, but it can bring good growth and change.

Jackie: Do not take criticism personally and do take it to the Lord. And realize that not everybody is going to love your husband.

Cynthia: First, be secure in your relationship with God. Second, ask Him for a discerning heart to judge the motives of people who criticize (1 Kings 3:9). Third, always direct the person to deal with your husband. Fourth, break the habit of listening to criticism, before it breaks you.

Vicki: Let your husband's problems be his, not yours. Encourage him. Let him talk about his feelings. Feel his hurt. Affirm him in his call and abilities and the Lord's sufficiency. Otherwise, stay out of it!

For Personal Meditation & Group Discussion

1. Consider the psalmist's experience of criticism in Psalms 31:18, 55:21, 56:5, 59:12-13, and 109:3. Do you identify with his thoughts and feelings?

2. Meditate on the wisdom of Psalm 49:3, Proverbs 8:8, 12:18, 16:24, 17:27, 24:26 (!), 26:4, Ephesians 4:15, 4:29 and James 1:19. What principles do you glean?

3. A comment from A. W. Tozer provides rock-solid confidence: *The truest thing about you is what God says about you.* Read Psalm 119:160 and then list how God sees us in Christ.

4. Some criticism is valid; it depends on the source, according to Proverbs 27:6. How do you respond to valid criticism?

Dear Friend,

For fun, being criticized ranks right up there with having teeth extracted without novocaine. I know I'm like Mama Bear when somebody messes with my cubs or man! So I'm not surprised that the issue of dealing with criticism comes up again and again as I talk with people married to ministry leaders.

In the panel discussion printed above, a subject that didn't come up in our interview is what I call vague criticism. By vague criticisms I mean the "you're-not-enough" stuff: loving enough, sincere enough, spiritual enough. Or maybe it's the "you're-too" stuff: too pushy, too proud, too shy.

I've found that many of Satan's accusations are of the vague variety. He tends to traffic in the not-enough and too-much type of indictment. Such vague charges are impossible to confront adequately because they always leave us ignorant or a bit confused about what precisely is problematic in our behaviors and attitudes.

On the other hand, we can get a handle on specific criticism. We know precisely what the perceived problem is when a person says, "When I talk to you, you don't look me in the eye and give me your full attention." Or, "I don't think a pastor's family should drive a fancy car." A specific complaint may or may not have merit, but at least you know what the expectation of the complainer is and can deal with it accordingly.

In my experience the Holy Spirit is specific when He convicts of sin. He points out that I exaggerated the facts or spoke unkindly or swore with my car horn or was not depending on God. When I confess my sin, it's specific confession based on

His letting me know precisely where I grieved Him and the area in which I need His help to change.

Through the years I've learned a way to treat vague criticism. I always ask for specific examples. "Could you give me an example of when I was too/not enough?" The answer to that question has either enlightened me with tangible evidence or quieted my criticizer, who lacked a solid basis for the criticism. Another way to probe is to ask, "How would I act/be if I were more/less as you'd like me to be?" Again, the complaint may or may not lack merit, but you'll know what you're confronting.

May you find a safe person to vent with when the heat is really on. Everybody needs a listening ear attached to a person who knows how to keep confidential what you say.

Warmly,

Pamela

14

Mothering Can Make You Hurt All Over

Christian leaders' kids are ordinary kids who, unfortunately, are apt to receive greater scrutiny than other children. Perhaps only politicians' kids have to put up with similar public attention. Children of doctors, lawyers, and postal workers (me) just don't carry the same burden of special expectations because of who their parents are.

The unwritten rule says a pastor's kids must be exemplary. We know, however, that kids don't always behave and believe just the way their parents — or church members — want. Some, in fact, are spiritually wayward or rebellious.

What follows comes from one who is a mother of two young adults (one homemade and one adopted) who has experienced pain in parenting. The latter fact gave me the dubious distinction of being invited to a seminary to do a workshop on "When Children Disappoint You." I'd love *not* to be qualified to speak to that subject!

Myths about Children

Some of our disappointment as parents is intensified because of myths about childrearing.

Myth #1: Children are blank slates. Wrong! Children are born with some givens. We've heard mothers say, "My kids had unique personalities right from the start." Just as children are born with certain physical characteristics, they also come into the world with certain temperaments, predispositions, strengths, and weaknesses. Children have some writing on their slate when we get them, and we'll never erase it any more than we'll change their eye color.

Myth #2: Good parents have good kids; bad parents have bad kids. Children think that good things happen to good people, and bad things happen to bad people. (That's why abused children assume they're bad.) When we become adults, we put away such childish thinking. Neglectful and abusive parents sometimes have children who become productive, admirable citizens. Pretty good parents sometimes have children who become criminals. That's reality.

Myth #3: Love conquers all. Love can beget love. Even perfect love, however, can be rejected. God's first children lived in perfect love in Eden's perfect environment, yet Adam and Eve disobeyed Him. Jesus loved enough to die for His friends, but Judas betrayed and Peter denied Him. No, dispensing love in huge doses doesn't automatically result in good kids.

Myth #4: Preachers' and other Christian leaders' kids are the worst. I can't believe people make such a ridiculous statement, but I've heard it. It isn't worth a comment.

A Parent's Influence

None of this means that we parents don't have an impact on our children. The quality of our parenting matters. Loved children generally grow into adults capable of giving and receiving love. Children who are encouraged in school often end up satisfactorily educated. Children who see Christ in their godly parents often establish a personal relationship with Him.

Studies show that parents who love, nurture, and respect their children, while setting appropriate limits and disciplining them fairly and consistently, tend to produce more mentally healthy and socially responsible kids than do uninvolved, dictatorial, or harshly critical parents. When parents provide a good example, lots of affection, and effective discipline, their children often respect and accept their values.

Thus the biblical writer penned, "Train a child in the way he should go, and when he is old he will not turn from it" (Prov. 22:6). This verse is not a promise. It's a proverb, a general expression about something that's generally — but not always — true. Sadly, many have stretched their faith to the breaking point because they've incorrectly interpreted this proverb as a promise, or else they've wallowed in guilt based on the assumption they've failed to train their child properly.

Children Have Wills

The reason pretty good (none is perfect) parents have no guarantee of producing godly offspring is that children have wills. They make choices. They decide to obey or to disobey, to comply or rebel. That's the way God made them.

When parents are physically bigger than a child, they can enforce their will in some areas. They can put a baby in a crib, and he's stuck there — like it or not. They can deliver a second-grader to school even though she'd rather not be there.

But even when a child is smaller, there's a limit to what parents can make him do. How do you force a child to eat against his will, apart from abuse? Can anything other than a hit on the head with a ball bat make a child go to sleep? (I can't make myself go to sleep some nights, and I can't make a child go to sleep on demand.)

The stronger a child's will, the more inventive and persistent she is in devising ways to circumvent our demands and wishes. The older the child, the less control we have.

Directing vs. Breaking the Will

The solution is not to break a child's will. Adults whose wills have been broken or severely crippled in childhood are pitiful adults. Children need a healthy ability to make choices and set boundaries if they are to assume appropriate responsibility as godly adults. So parents do better to think in terms of directing a child's will.

According to Proverbs 21:1, our Father does this. "The king's heart is in the hand of the Lord; he directs it like a watercourse wherever he pleases." Commenting on this, Matthew Henry wrote:

> God can change men's minds, can turn them from that which they seemed most intent upon, as the husbandman, by canals and gutters, turns the water through his grounds, which does not alter the nature of the water, nor put any force upon it, anymore than God's providence does upon the native freedom of man's will, but directs the course of it to serve His own purpose.

Remember the story of the kid standing up in the back seat of the car? Mom told him to sit down. He refused. She pulled the car to the side of the road and calmly said the car wouldn't move until he complied. At that, the child sat down, buckled up, and said, "I may be sitting down on the outside but inside I'm standing straight up!" Given the alternative, he changed his behavior, but that didn't change his attitude or inclination a smidgen.

This reminds me of the saying, "You can lead a horse to water, but you can't make him drink." Given enough salty food, however, he may be powerfully motivated to drink. In many cases, the most parents can do is provide incentive for their children to follow their direction, but obedience is a child's choice.

Don't Carry Your Kid's Backpack

Wise parents know what they can and can't do with their children. This previews the discussion of boundaries in Chapter 25.

Counselors describe skin as the boundary surrounding an individual's property. What's within one's skin — feelings, thoughts, wants and wishes, choices, behaviors, gifts and talents, beliefs, likes and dislikes, attitudes, values, and our standard of what behaviors we'll accept or tolerate from others and what we won't — is his or her responsibility.

How children feel, think, choose, behave and believe, and what they dislike and value, is inside their boundaries. As much as we parents would like to determine their feelings, choices and so on, we can't.

Though we love our wayward or rebellious children dearly, we do well to understand that we can't fix, heal, rescue, or save them. Once children reach their late teens (and maybe sooner), the best parents can do is pray for them fervently, assure them of their love, wisely draw appropriate boundaries, and release them to the consequences of their choices and God's love and discipline.

Carry Your Load Responsibly

We as parents must draw appropriate boundaries in dealing with our children. Early in my process of dealing with a child who made foolish, harmful, and ungodly decisions, I consciously, deliberately distinguished between my boundaries and hers. I wanted to be clear on what I could control (me, not her), what was my responsibility (my choices and behaviors, not hers), and for what God would hold me accountable (myself, not her).

We parents decide what we will or won't tolerate. (I won't tolerate having drugs in my house.) We choose how to honor God with our money. (I won't give my child money to enable her to do something harmful, illegal, or sinful.) We prayerfully decide our values. (I value trust, and trust is earned.)

We own our feelings. No matter how wayward our children are, our disappointment, fear, shame, anger, and guilt are ours to deal with, not theirs. It's not our children's duty to "straighten up and fly right" just so we'll feel better.

Our heavenly Father grieves over His wayward children, but we do not embarrass Him. Likewise, we hurting parents do well to refuse shame for our children's choices. We do this even when others may wrongly hold us liable for their behavior.

I believe we may, despite our rebellious children, hear the Father say some day, "Well done, good and faithful parent! Through the difficulties, you prayed and loved well, and you trusted My goodness in your grief."

For Personal Meditation & Group Discussion

1. Read Hosea 11:1-11. Either rewrite or tell to one other person (paraphrase) this passage in your own words. As you do, feel the Father's heartbreak over Israel. Hurt often erupts in anger; what did the wrathful Father consider doing to punish His children? What kept Him from permanently writing them off? What were the consequences of His children's sin? Has your hurt as a parent helped you understand God's hurt when you sin?

2. Meditate on Proverbs 19:19. In place of "hot-tempered man," insert alcoholic son, promiscuous daughter, or whatever is your situation. Have you rescued your child again and again and again? Why is that unhelpful?

3. If you know specific ways you've sinned against your child, is 1 John 1:9 still true? Can you accept God's forgiveness?

4. God never expected you to be a perfect parent. According to Romans 8:1, does God condemn your imperfection? According to Revelation 12:10, who's to blame for self-condemning feelings? James 4:7 explains how to deal with him. How did Jesus do this in His temptation?

5. Read 2 Corinthians 1:3-5. Has God comforted you? If so, how will you pass on the comfort to other hurting parents?

Dear Friend,

Parental pain. What an unhappy topic. The problem of wayward or rebellious children, however, is one many of us confront. Believing Jesus' promise that truth sets us free, we do well to bring this dark subject into the light.

When I first wrote of this matter, my then 21-year-old daughter lived about ten miles away. She was a never-married welfare mother. After months of homelessness, she had settled into a wretched apartment in a house that also was home to a couple of thieves, an aging prostitute, and a violent alcoholic. It's now about eight years later, and her parental rights have been terminated. For a few years she disappeared, and I had no clue where she was.

Our daughter received the best parenting my husband and I knew how to give her. We laced her childhood with earnest, constant prayer and sought God's guidance on how to love and discipline her. When her problems became obvious, we got her the best help we could afford, including time in three different psychiatric hospitals and an extended stay in a children's residential treatment center.

I've told people that the difference between the grief of a mother whose child has died and that of a mother of a rebellious child is somewhat parallel to the difference between the way a divorcée and a widow are treated. Widows and death-bereaved parents generally receive material, emotional, and spiritual support from people. Divorcées and we parents of rebellious children are often blamed ("What did you do wrong?") and held totally responsible ("When are you going to fix this?"). Since our children aren't buried, ours is a grief without closure.

Every year our daughter's life seems to take some new and complex twist that breaks our hearts. We at times have felt like players in an ongoing soap opera with a rotten script. The best we can do is live through the situation relying on God's wisdom, expressing Jesus' love, and acting with an integrity that doesn't violate our boundaries or our daughter's.

Now you understand I don't write from an ivory tower. I know intimately the pain that comes when dreams for a responsible, godly son or daughter have not been realized. I know the comfort of releasing a child to the tender mercies of our Heavenly Father.

Warmly,

Pamela

15
Hurting Moms Speak Out

Let me introduce you to ministry moms whom I'll call Abby, Barb, and Connie — not their real names. (I do this to protect their children's privacy, which neither they nor I care to violate.) In a candid interview they talked of their spiritually wayward or rebellious kids.

PHH: Will you share something of your story of pain with a child?

Abby: At 16, my son became angry with God. He watched his father go through a serious illness and decided that, if God would allow this bad thing to happen to a good man, then he didn't want anything to do with serving God. He went through ten years of open rebellion, which involved alcohol, drugs, being in and out of jail, and finally a three-year stay in the state prison.

Barb: Our son began to rebel at 14. This rebellion was aided and abetted by a deacon who thought it was helpful to hold up his son, who was the same age, as an example to our son. Our boy ran away from home the day after this man pulled him aside at church and lectured him. A year after our son graduated from high school, his girlfriend became pregnant. He took responsibility to support the child and the mother when their baby was a year old. (Her parents wouldn't permit the marriage until the girl was 18.) He had a hard time keeping a job for several years.

Connie: When our adopted daughter became a teen, she was so disruptive to the church youth group that she was asked not to attend it. She disregarded our rules and refused to cooperate with them. She used drugs. She still insists that doing so is all right. At one point we felt we had to practice tough love and have her move out of our home.

PHH: Hurting moms often deal with guilt, shame, anger, fear, and spiritual doubts. Have you?

Connie: Yes. Though we could look at our other child and see that he was doing well, it was hard for me not to think that we as parents had done something wrong because of our daughter's problems. I felt this even though I believed we had been good, consistent, and loving parents.

Barb: I felt like I had failed our son terribly. He suffered from an extremely low self-image, and that felt like my fault. When things with him were at the lowest (lost a job, conflict in his marriage, drinking), I asked him what I had done to make his life turn out like it had. He responded that it was not what we, his parents, did or the mistakes we made. He said he had sinned by his own choice.

Abby: I struggled daily with the guilt that I had failed as a mother. No matter how hard I tried to convince myself that my son had a mind of his own and was making wrong choices on his own, and that I had taught him right from wrong, I thought somewhere along the way I had to have failed him. I felt both fear and anger. I feared for his future and was angry at what he was doing to himself. I feared for our future as a family and was angry at what he was doing to us. I feared for our future as servants of Jesus Christ and was angry at what he was doing to our ministry.

PHH: What I hear is that painful feelings come with the territory for moms of wayward children. Such feelings can cripple us. So, how did you survive with your faith and sanity intact?

Barb: I reminded myself of Paul's statement that I couldn't change the past. "Forgetting the things that are behind, I press on."

Abby: My survival is only to the credit of Jesus Christ. He carried me through the tough times by the strength of the Holy Spirit and His Word. He placed a wonderful Christian counselor in my path, who was trained in dealing with people at the end of their own strength. This man directed me back to the source of strength — Jesus Christ. God also placed in my path people who had been through similar pain and survived. They were of great encouragement to me.

PHH: Some in the Christian community say that counseling and support groups are unspiritual. What I hear you saying, Abby, is that God used other people to help you. It's helped me to have Christian sisters and brothers walk alongside as I've gone through tough stuff, and I believe there's strong biblical support for this.

Abby: Yes. You need to share your pain. Seek out people who love the Lord and have been through some of life's trials. People who will allow you to be honest, take your mask off, and become real. Many times I could not even pray, and these people interceded for me.

Barb: I think we need to find someone to be our special confidant and encourager. My sister was mine. When we share our problems with another, it is easier to pray about it. That may sound backward, but sometimes we are afraid to tell God our true feelings.

Connie: I met once a month with other mothers who had rebellious kids. This group helped me maintain hope. In fact, my word to any parent facing this situation is to get some support from other people. Another thing that helped me was my decision not to take responsibility for my daughter's choices.

PHH: How did your churches respond to your situation?

Abby: Overall it was compassion and love. A few younger members were, as they put it, "concerned about the effect of our situation on the church." This devastated me! Many times I felt the best thing to do was to leave the ministry. But God always brought people who encouraged us to continue on.

Connie: Some in our church don't know anything about what we went through. Some who knew commended us for our openness. Some who knew ignored it. It never, however, became a matter for gossip.

Barb: The church we were in at the time seemed to ignore the situation. Maybe we didn't share enough. The next church we served has seen the changed life of our son and has rejoiced in the prodigal's return.

PHH: What would you say to other Christian women in

leadership who are experiencing what you have? Or what suggestions would you have for any who counsel hurting parents?

Connie: I'd remind them that we asked God to give us wisdom as we raised our children. I think we need to have confidence in the wisdom He gave us at the time.

Barb: Read the Psalms!

PHH: I'm glad you mentioned the Psalms. During a recent painful time I've prayed through Psalms from Eugene Peterson's The Message. His contemporary expressions of David's thoughts and feelings mirrored the rawness of my ordeal.

Abby: Yes, the Psalms were such an encouragement to me, also. Stay close to the Lord through His Word. Romans 8:28 was my source of survival many, many times. The one thing I did know was that I loved the Lord and that we were called according to His purpose. "As for me and my household, we will serve the Lord" (Josh. 24:15) reminded me that we had other children who needed us to carry on, to be strong, to continue serving the Lord. We had to set an example for them, with or without our son.

PHH: Any final thoughts as we close this interview?

Barb: Trials because of our children will be redeemed and used by God. I see this when God uses us with other teens.

Abby: God brought people to us who were hurting because of their children. Moms felt comfortable coming to me with their heartache because I was real. I could empathize with them. I began to speak to groups of women, sharing my heartache and source of strength and letting them know that there is hope in the midst of pain.

Barb: I want to say there's hope! Our story has a good ending.

Our son and his wife have returned to the Lord. Both are Awana workers and Sunday school teachers. Their three children (two are teens) have accepted the Lord as Savior. My son attended Promise Keepers.

For Personal Meditation & Group Discussion

1. How do you feel about pastors' wives being as open as Amy, Barb, and Connie were in this interview? Would you feel free sharing the struggles you face with some trusted members of your congregation or organization? Why or why not?

2. How can we share relationship pain in order to gain the needed support and comfort of our Christian family, while at the same time protecting the privacy of the one causing the pain?

3. How do you explain the fact that mothers tend to take responsibility for their child's or children's wrong choices and behaviors?

4. Read some of Psalms from *The Message,* such as 6, 10, 12, 13, and 22. Have you ever spoken this honestly with God about your feelings? If not, why not?

5. If you're hurting because of a child or for any other reason, write a psalm in the style of David to express your thoughts and feelings to God.

Dear Friend,

Susanna Wesley had 19 children; nine of them died before she did. Of course, we know of John and Charles Wesley, but what have you heard about Hetty, who broke her mother's heart? Susanna wrote to her brother:

> Oh, brother! Happy, thrice happy are you... that buried your children in infancy! Secure from temptation, secure from guilt, secure from want or shame, or loss of friends! They are safe beyond the realm of pain or sense of misery.... Believe me, sire, it is better to mourn ten children dead than one living; and I have buried many. (From *Susanna Wesley* by Arnold A. Dallimore, p. 102.)

I'm glad I could share with you the wisdom and insights of three vulnerable pastors' wives whose interview appears in this chapter. One interviewee expressed a hope that those of you who have not gone through the valley with your children will gain sensitivity and compassion for members in your churches who are parents in pain.

I remember vividly when my daughter turned my world upside down in the most horrific way. We cared for her daughter, my granddaughter, for 11 months — more than half her little life at the time. Then we were forced to return that precious baby to our daughter. We observed 16 months of this little one's neglect and abuse, but found we could not get child protective services in our county to take our concerns seriously.

I was grateful that few (though there were some) Job's comforters came my way positing simplistic, unhelpful answers.

More often, the love and support of friends and colleagues deeply touched me. I identify with Abby, who in her interview said that there were times she couldn't pray, but she had friends who could and did.

It reminds me of hearing a speaker once say that when she ran out of hope, a friend of hers said, "That's okay. I still have some, and I'll lend you mine for as long as you need it." That's acceptance and compassion.

Oh, yes, my story has a happy ending. The day came when we adopted our granddaughter. (And we'll always be 50 years older than she.) I rejoice in this example of God's rescue of our grandchild; I'm still waiting for God's intervention in our daughter's life.

If you're still in the midst of grief about a disobedient child, understand that you may never have the answer to all the whys. We won't necessarily have all the answers this side of heaven. I've found I don't need reasons and explanations as much as I simply need to rest in my Abba Father.

Warmly,

Pamela

16
Love, Honor & Set Good Boundaries

In Belva Plain's novel, *Whispers,* Robert's wife battering escalates as steadily as his climb up the corporate ladder of a Fortune 500 company. He criticizes Lynn, blames her unfairly, frightens her with his rage, leaves bruises on her arms where he's grabbed her, and throws her forcefully onto their bed. Always it's Lynn's fault. Could he help it if she fell into a thorn bush while dodging an expected blow — all because she "stupidly" thought his raised hand aimed at her face meant he intended to hit her? Though the abuse is always Lynn's fault, Robert nevertheless offers profuse apologies each time and vows he'll never get violent with her again.

Lynn keeps quiet about her abuse. Though her kids ask perceptive questions, she lies about what they plainly see. Her sister notices the telltale signs, and Lynn denies any problem. Lynn covers and makes excuses and feels lonely and ashamed as she tries to protect her husband's reputation and her family's uneasy stability. Ultimately, however, she can't hide the truth from others or herself. Robert loses his job and his marriage as a result.

More Fact than Fiction

This kind of thing doesn't happen just in novels. It happens everyday even in Christian families — even in pastors' families. A pastor opens a gash on his son's head and lies about it to his wife: "No, I didn't hit him; he bumped his head." Christian men frighten their wives and kids with their temper tantrums. They unsettle their family with punitive emotional distance that keeps the family walking on eggshells and makes their wives feel like married singles. They hold a wife or child responsible for their choices and behaviors and moods. They lie and cheat and swear and covet.

Christian leaders can be addicted to legal and illegal drugs, food, and alcohol. They can be workaholics robbing their families of deserved time, energy, and positive attention. They can be control freaks expecting family members to bow to their whims and wishes, and meting out negative consequences if thwarted in getting their way.

Christian men can be snared by sexual misconduct ranging from pornography to sexual intercourse outside of marriage. A survey revealed that 12 percent of pastors admitted to having sex with a person other than their spouse; 39 percent felt sexual fantasies about a person other than their spouse were harmless. The percentage of those guilty of sexually inappropriate behavior other than intercourse is much higher than 12 percent obviously. All of us involved in counseling pastoral families know that an alarming number of pastors have gotten trapped in

Internet porn.

In other words, just about every sin one sees among unbelievers is being committed inside the church, even by some pastors. Those of us who don't believe in sinless perfection this side of heaven shouldn't be surprised.

Defending Against the Truth

Often when a wife confronts her pastor-husband with his sinful behavior, the response is denial. Nope, it didn't happen. Nope, it isn't happening. You're too suspicious if you could accuse me of that. You have an overactive imagination. "Denial isn't just a river in Egypt" goes the joke, but such denial is no laughing matter.

Or the response may be minimization. C'mon, it's no big deal. Or, you're making a mountain out of a molehill. Or, I may seem a tad out of control at the moment, but as soon as this stress passes I'll be my usual wonderful self again. Or, I've got to spend time with her; it's my duty as her pastor.

Usually there's some passing the buck. You're the one to blame — if only you were more (or less) this or that then I wouldn't be doing what I'm doing. Sometimes the response is *yes — but*, as in, Yes, I was guilty of that, but not anymore; I've conquered this. Occasionally this is true, but too often such claims to spiritual victory are just wishful thinking on the offender's part.

Co-conspiring in Sin

When a woman considers the possibility that her pastor-husband is involved in sin, or he is sitting on temptation's slippery slope, sometimes *she* does the denying. Surely her godly man couldn't possibly be guilty of such wrongdoing. She may work hard not to see the obvious signs that something is wrong.

Sometimes a wife believes that her concerns deserve airing, so she confronts her husband. If he doesn't admit to her accusations, she may quickly buy his explanations, excuses, denial, minimization, and profession of victory over sin. She desperately wants to believe she has nothing to worry about; so, if she seriously doubts his statements, she suppresses them and keeps quiet about them.

When another is involved in her husband's sin, for example the "other woman," a pastor's wife sometimes puts all the blame on the "seductress." If it weren't for her.... She overlooks the obvious — any relationship, healthy or unhealthy, takes two. Or she blames herself: "If only I were a better cook or housekeeper. I'm not submissive enough or sexy enough." She forgets that even if her shortcomings may contribute to the strength of her husband's temptation to sin, he alone chooses whether or not to yield to temptation. If she needs to confess and repent of sins, she needs to do so; but she violates his boundaries when she accepts blame for his sins, no matter how convincingly she may hear outer voices or her inner voices say that the whole problem is her fault.

Occasionally, both husband and wife fully admit to the fact of inappropriate or wrong behavior that's ongoing, but they close ranks to keep this secret. Such action is understandable since a pastor can lose his reputation, his job, and his home if his sin or character flaw becomes public. Astonishingly, some women actually believe that God would rather they enable a husband to continue in his sin than take strong action to stop the sin. Some truly think that God expects them to overlook a pastor-husband's sin so they don't jeopardize his ministry in any way. As my colleague, Rich Massey, says, "Wives can become co-conspirators in their husband's sin."

What's a Wife to Do?

Don't misunderstand me. We all sin. We all have character flaws. We all have lots of healing, recovery, and growing to do. I'm not talking about informing the church deacons that your husband is a perfect grouch after a short night of sleep. What I am talking about is sins and character flaws and compulsions that have the potential to destroy a man's marriage and ministry.

So how does a woman deal with the serious character flaws and sins of a pastor-husband? Let me give you a few hypothetical cases that may sound real, because they're unfortunately too common.

Case #1: *"My husband's anger is beginning to really scare me. He's actually broken things when he got mad."*

First, understand that you're dealing with abuse. (Psychological abuse is controlling another by fear.) You must set a boundary immediately. Let him know you'll no longer tolerate his out-of-control, ungodly rage. It must stop. Immediately. You do this not only for your sake but also for the sake of your children, who are imprinting this model on their souls. Also, you need to understand that uncontrolled rage often escalates into physical abuse; throwing things becomes throwing people. Ask your husband to get counseling to help him deal with this problem.

"He'll just tell me he'll pray about it, and we should just trust God to deal with this."

It's not a matter of either praying or getting help. A both-and approach is important — just as we pray for healing and get antibiotics for pneumonia. Often we can't pray intelligently about our deepest problems because we don't have a clue as to what's at the root of them. Counseling can provide the insight about what we need to pray and trust God for. Anger isn't the problem; it's a symptom of something bigger.

If your husband refuses counseling, you need counseling to gain support for setting no-violence boundaries in your home. One of the things you must do is this: When he rages, get you and your children out of the room or out of the house immediately. You may want to set a consequence, telling him that the next time objects fly in your house you will talk to his ecclesiastical superior about the problem and seek his intervention to save your marriage and ministry.

Case #2: *"A woman in our church is trying to attract my husband's attention in an unhealthy way. In his pocket I found a note she wrote; it said she's falling in love with him. My husband says she's crazy and I don't need to worry about her."*

Yes, you do need to worry. Since we all crave affection, loving attention is flattering and can be very tempting to any of us. Your husband needs to show the woman's note to the elders and tell them to deal with this to protect him, you, your family, the church, and even the woman herself. You have a right to insist that he do this.

Case #3: *"I never would have thought a pastor would treat his kids like my husband does ours. He yells at, ridicules, and criticizes them; he calls them derogatory names. They never meet his perfectionist standards. They hide in their bedrooms when they hear his car pull into the garage."*

You're the mother; your responsibility is to protect your kids from emotional abuse. Words can harm as much as a whip; they can leave lasting scars. You need to develop a plan for stopping this verbal violence. The plan might include 1) telling your husband that the way he's treating your children is not acceptable, 2) calling a family meeting where the kids can express with grace and truth what his verbal abuse is doing to them, 3) letting you husband know that when he cuts loose with a sinful mouth that you and the children will leave the room until he can speak with respect and maturity, and 4) asking that the family go to a counselor to find a solution. If your husband refuses personal or family counseling, then you must get help for yourself to provide ongoing encouragement and insight on how to handle this situation.

By the way, never excuse your pastor-husband's wrong behavior to your children, or you're teaching them to excuse sin. Never, never, never confuse showing unconditional love with overlooking transgressions. God loves unconditionally, and He acknowledges, rebukes, and hates sin. That's our model.

Case #4: *"I believe my husband is having an emotional affair with a staff woman. I don't know if there's any physical involvement. He says she's just a very good friend; there's nothing romantic about it. I don't know whether to believe him or not. He knows I'm upset that they meet alone, but he says the problem is that I don't trust him as I should."*

Even if you have no tangible evidence to confirm your suspicions, take your intuition very seriously. Our spirits can pick up clues totally missed by our rational faculties. If your husband's excuses sound lame, if his explanations don't compute, if the relationship feels wrong, you're not crazy to feel alarmed. Don't accept too quickly that it's all your imagination.

There may be nothing sexual in the relationship, but such a "friendship" unchecked may end up in a full-blown sexual affair. Neither he nor you dare risk that. You have the right — even the obligation — to set boundaries to protect your marriage. One is that he may not be alone with this woman. He may not call her on the phone unless you are present. He may not send her any letter that is not typed by the church secretary. (If the woman is the church secretary, she or your husband may need to find another job.) If he balks at these limits, then he values the "friend" and his freedom to indulge his own desires more than he values you and your feelings. Ask him to talk to another pastor, his ecclesiastical superior, or a Christian counselor to bring a needed objective third party into the process of dealing with this problem. If he refuses to cut off the relationship or to seek outside help, then you contact an outside third party who can provide help.

"He's such a proud man, I don't think I could do that to him. If I were to tell anybody about this, my husband would be furious."

You're probably dealing with his shame, not pride. Regardless, you need to be clear that setting boundaries and seeking help are things you do *for* your husband and marriage, not something you do *to* him. Make no mistake about it, you can deal with this problem now or you almost certainly will have to deal with it later when it's escalated, blown up in your face, and created a scandal. Realize that the damage you feel to your soul by what's happening now is *nothing* compared to the destruction to your marriage and ministry if this inappropriate relationship isn't stopped immediately. Furthermore, an affair could destroy the church if the woman later sues on the basis of clergy malpractice. As Rich Massey says, "A pastor's wife needs to believe her marriage is a *very big deal,* because it is." You have a right and obligation to protect or salvage your marriage by any godly means.

Case #5: *"My husband confessed he used to visit pornographic web sites, but he assures me that's all in the past. He says he's repented and God's forgiven him. He acts like it was something minor when, in reality, I'm devastated by this violation of our marriage.*

Also, how can I be sure he's no longer involved in porn?"

Porn isn't minor; it's deeply wounded you and your marriage. I believe people who feel deeply wounded by another need to lay out four facts for the offender. 1) This is what you did — the facts. 2) This is how those actions made me feel, using the most descriptive words possible. 3) This is the ongoing impact in my life. 4) This is what I need you to do to restore our relationship.

Using the Internet porn example, a wife shares the facts: 1) You went outside our marriage to have your sexual needs met. Your involvement in Internet porn supported an evil industry that degrades women as sex objects rather than as persons made in God's image. You violated your marriage vows. You sinned against God. 2) I feel shocked and horrified by this. I feel physically ill. I can't sleep. I could cry for a month and not wash the hurt away. I feel humiliated even though I didn't do anything to be ashamed of. I feel like I'm going to die of sadness. I'm so angry I'd like to hurt you. 3) I don't trust you any more. How can I be sure you won't do this again? I can't get into bed with you without my imagination running wild about what vile things you saw. And I wonder how I compare with your fantasies. The worst part is, you're my pastor as well as my husband; and I can't respect your spiritual leadership. 4) I want our marriage to survive this. I want restoration of trust and respect and love. For that to happen I need to know you truly understand the damage you've done to my soul. I need to see a spirit of genuine repentance and remorse. I need for the two of us to go to counseling to make sure that we've dealt with the issues that led to this. I want us to be involved with another couple or two in an accountability group. And I need you to give me time for God to work the process of forgiveness in me. Don't expect this wound to heal overnight; it will take time. You will need to be patient with me.

Motivating to Do Right

I've met many pastors. I respect and appreciate them. I pray you have every reason to love and honor your pastor-husband. Spouses owe that to each other. At the same time, I'm not naive, and you need not be either, about the reality that good men (and women) need others to set appropriate boundaries. As wives, one of our jobs is to protect our marriages and homes and to do what we can to rouse our men to love and good deeds (Heb. 10:24).

For Personal Meditation & Group Discussion

1. Do you differentiate between garden-variety flaws, sins and significant character flaws and ministry-destroying sins? If so, what are the differences?

2. List the kinds of sins in leaders that are destructive of their ministries and marriages. How can or should a pastor's wife deal with such sins? What would keep you from setting appropriate boundaries in regard to your husband's sin?

3. Study the account of Ananias and Sapphira in Acts 5. What could Sapphira have done not to be a co-conspirator in sin with her husband? How do you know God held her as accountable as he?

4. How do you think Matthew 18:15-17 applies to a woman when the offender is her pastor-husband?

4. Read *Boundaries in Marriage* by Henry Cloud and John Townsend to learn how to set God-honoring limits that protect and enhance your marriage.

5. According to Galatians 6:1, what qualities do you need when you attempt to restore one caught in sin? What do you think it means to be "caught in" sin?

6. Hebrews 10:24 speaks of our responsibility to "spur one another on toward love and good deeds." Write down some ways to apply this command in the context of a marriage relationship.

Love, Honor & Set Good Boundaries

Dear Friend,

Writing a chapter addressing a wife's need to deal with a pastor's character flaws and sins that threaten her marriage and ministry distresses me. I had so much internal resistance to the whole idea; but a colleague said, "If you'll speak to this, many women will rise up and call you blessed." I hope he didn't mean what my southern friends mean when they say they "got blessed out"!

My conviction is that God calls a sin a sin because of its destructive affect on individuals and their relationships. I don't think there's such a thing as a victimless sin.

The sinner is the first and foremost victim. Not only does sin erect a barrier between the sinner and God, sin builds a barrier between the sinner and her or his authentic self. Sin brings guilt and shame, an inability to live at peace inside one's own skin.

Of course, there are other victims. Our spouses usually bear consequences of our sins. So do our children. A child's earliest concept of God is often based on a parent, and the spiritual affect is only compounded if dad is a pastor who speaks for God every time he enters the pulpit. A pastor-father's sin can do long-term damage to a child's relationship to our Abba Father.

I've also observed that when one consistently sins against another and the victim doesn't set boundaries, the sinner loses respect and comes to hate the victim for letting him get away with being his worst self. We may dislike boundaries, but we also need them the way we need painted lines on the highway to feel safe. As spouses, we must believe that to set limits on a mate's destructive behavior is an act of love.

It's the rare woman who can do this all by herself. Most of us need another to provide support and insight as we set appropriate, protective boundaries. I pray you have a discreet older friend who will walk with you through this process and keep confidential what you share. (A great definition of such a friend is a woman who knows the worst stuff about your husband and still treats him with respect and kindness.) A counselor can provide great coaching and must keep confidential what you tell him or her.

Warmly,

Pamela

Part 4

Relating to Ministry: A One-of-a-Kind Servant of God

17

Have You Joined the Church?

You're in your present church because it extended a call to your husband to be its pastor. Cosgrove and Hatfield, authors of *Church Conflicts,* say that extending a call doesn't necessarily mean a church is granting a pastor the *right* to minister. It very well could be simply inviting a pastor to *earn the right* to minister.

I suspect there's a correlation for the pastor's wife. You're not automatically given the right to have a significant place of respect in your church; you have only the opportunity to earn the congregation's love and trust.

Whether you and your husband are allowed to do what you believe God called you to do in your church, when you accepted its call, may depend largely on how quickly and how well you join the church family. I'm *not* talking about joining the church, which is a fairly simple process. I'm talking about the more difficult task of becoming a valued, accepted, and loved part of the church family.

Something Like Adoption

When Lowell and I had been a family for seven years, I gave birth to our first child, a son. Two years later our family of three added another member. We adopted a baby girl.

There's a difference between bringing a homemade baby from the hospital and bringing an adopted baby home from the agency. I could look at Toby and see miniature features from both sides of our family; Noelle looked like neither of us. I'd had nine months to bond with Toby while I carried him in my womb and during those intense first days spent in the hospital with him. When we picked up Noelle, she was truly a little stranger to us. I had to get to know her and begin the bonding process in a way that was not true for our son.

Unless you planted your present church, the church family was already established when you and your husband arrived on the scene. The members knew each other and had a history together. They could articulate the stories and traditions and explain the roles and rules operating in that family system. You were strangers, outsiders to the insider group. While you had some bonds with your new church because of your common faith in Christ and membership in the universal Family of God, strong bonds to that specific local family of believers had yet to be forged. You were the adopted children, so to speak, coming into an existing family.

Adoptions Don't Always Work

After many years of counseling, our daughter (then an adolescent) was admitted to a psychiatric hospital. She was treated for many problems, one of which was her inability to bond or attach. (I believe that prenatal damage destroyed her ability to form attachments.) In one session with our family, the counselor said to our daughter, "Your family adopted you, but you never adopted your family." In the parlance of social workers, this was "a failed adoption."

Some adoptions don't work because the adoptive parents decide that the child isn't right for them and their family for one reason or another. Maybe the parents don't adjust to the special needs of the child; they may be incapable of dealing with them. Sometimes, despite the best efforts of the adoptive couple, it's the child who doesn't adjust to the family.

The same kind of thing can happen when a pastoral family attempts to become a part of a local church family — the "adoption" doesn't seem to work. The problem may be that the church family is closed to what the pastor and his wife have to offer. Perhaps they're not enough like the dear family members who just moved away — the former ministry couple. Maybe they want the new ministry couple to be what they aren't and can't be; the pastor and his wife don't have the gifts and personality to fit the church's expectations.

Or it can work the other way. The ministry couple may have solid, perhaps even biblical, reasons why they won't buy into the church family's roles and rules. They see the church family system as fundamentally dysfunctional or carnal, and they find deep resistance when they confront that unhealthy or ungodly system. Or perhaps the pastoral couple was deeply hurt in the last church, so they've got their guard up; and their unhealed trust wound keeps them from taking the new congregation into their hearts and home. They fear getting hurt again. Or maybe the ministry couple is convinced that to lead requires maintaining distance between the leader and the led, between clergy and laity. (When I was a young I remember a pastor's wife who always referred to her husband as "Rev. Patterson.")

Whatever the cause of distance between the ministry couple and the congregation, tension and even conflict — along with blaming — often result when a warm, accepting connection never developed.

The Nature of Families

Let's face it, there are families and there are families. Some families are warm, accepting, nurturing, and honest. They welcome a stranger into the family circle with open arms; they "adopt" new members (like in-laws!) graciously. They respect and value individual members. They're patient with mistakes and offer forgiveness when offended.

Some families, on the other hand, can be difficult. They criticize, hurt, embarrass, and demean individuals in the family. Home isn't a haven of safety and security. Acceptance is conditional, based on performance. Strangers may become acquaintances, but rarely intimate friends and never "one of us."

Have You Joined the Church?

I'm making the assumption that you, as well as your husband, have been called by God to the particular church family of which you're now a part. You're not there by accident. God's sovereign plan is to use you in that place with those people to fulfill His grand mission.

If you don't adopt this family which God gave you, it's probable that the family will likewise never adopt you as a full-fledged member. If you keep your church family at a distance, you may have vision, motivation, gifts, resources, and skills up the wazoo, but never be given permission to use them and, thus, realize your goals for advancing God's kingdom. You may have all the right goals, do all the right things, and go through all the right motions, but never see the church family grow in quality and quantity as you'd like.

A leader — that's you — is a person of influence and impact. The degree of your connection will most likely determine the extent of your influence and impact. Dr. Howard Hendricks of Dallas Seminary said, "You can impress people at a distance; you can only impact them up close. The general principle is this: the closer the relationship, the greater the impact."

So it's not only appropriate but also imperative to ask yourself, "Have I personally, intentionally joined our church family? Have I fully embraced my family role in Christ as a sister to my age peers, a daughter or granddaughter to older women and men, and an aunt or even mother-figure to younger women?"

Joining through Affirmation and Identification

Whether or not your people will take you into their hearts, thus opening avenues for effective ministry, will almost certainly depend on whether you take them into your heart. You show you've done this by affirming and identifying with the church family. Cosgrove and Hatfield write:

> A newcomer cannot join without invitation and acceptance by the family.... But joining itself is something the newcomer must decide to do.... That response must include at least two elements of affiliation: affirmation and identification. Affirmation means expressing appreciation and praise to others for the things we value about them. Identification means discovering and matching similarities between ourselves and others (pp. 178-179).

What do affirming and identifying look like? It means not talking as if the area of the country in which the church is located is greatly defective compared to where you grew up or just came from. It means never making disparaging contrasts between the present congregation and a past one. It means never looking down your nose in arrogant superiority. It means finding all the good you can about the church, its members, its community, and its culture and expressing appreciation in ways that are heard. It may mean adjusting your dress and your customs, as foreign missionaries sometimes have to do, to adapt to the culture you hope to reach. (In some countries women don't wear slacks, so missionary women don't either.) It may mean taking up new hobbies and activities to create common ground.

Am I saying you should whittle vital aspects of your personality away to fit a mold? That you should gladly dispose of your own identity? Of course not. Your unique self with all your gifts and skills is God's gift to enrich your church family. At the same time, you must adventurously and joyfully embrace church members as God's enriching gift to you, your family, your community, and your world. Just as He wants to use you to help shape their lives; they are to help shape yours as well.

God gave you your church family. Accept them. Love them. Appreciate them. Enthusiastically adopt them as your own.

For Personal Meditation & Group Discussion

1. What "cross-cultural" adjustments, if any, have you had to make in your present church? How does this church's culture differ from others you've experienced? What roles has your church family assigned to you? To your husband? How well do they fit who you are? Do you deal with expectations contradictory to your understanding of God's will? Can you live with the rules of your church family without violating your integrity as a biblical Christian and the way God made you?

2. Read 1 Corinthians 9:19-23 and reflect on Paul's statement. What does that mean to you in your specific church situation?

3. Look up the word *incarnation* in the dictionary. Now read John 1:14 and Philippians 2:1-11. What did it mean for Jesus to join us, the human family?

4. What would it mean for you to have an incarnational relationship ("being Jesus with skin on") with your church family? How would joining your church family be an act of faith on your part?

Dear Friend,

Family. The Scripture brims with the concept. The Godhead is referred to in family terms as Father and Son. God officiated at the first marriage and ordered Adam and Eve to produce the first human, biological family. God set apart a family, Abraham's, through whom to bless the world. God prompted Paul to describe the church as a family relationship. God indeed "sets the lonely in families."

One of my dearest sisters in God's family was a pastor's wife. When she was battling cancer, Shannah and I talked many times. One of the last times we talked, Shannah expressed in many different ways how much she loved her church family. She mentioned how the church was growing. She told how much genuine care members showed one another. In case I missed the point, she said point blank to me: "I'm more convinced than ever that ministry is about relationships. It's not about putting on more and better programs. It's about loving people."

The message of 1 John is that love is the hallmark of the Christian. The way we witness to the reality that we follow Jesus is our love for His other followers. If we don't love, we're noisy and nothing, according to the Love Chapter.

It's easy to lose sight of that. We can give great attention to making sure people dot their theological I's and cross their theological T's just the way we do. We can spend lots of time reading books and attending seminars looking for programs and formats to promote church growth. We can sit in interminable committee meetings revising constitutions and bylaws, hoping that new structures will advance Christ's kingdom. Teaching doctrine, gaining skill, and organizing are good and necessary, but without love they don't accomplish much.

The church is a family, both nuclear (local) and extended (universal). Our role as ministry leaders is to love the family.

I'm not saying that's easy. Some family members are downright unlikable, though with God's grace they are lovable. Some do things that are inexcusable, but are forgivable by God's grace. Aren't you glad the ability to love and forgive doesn't originate in us? The kind of acceptance, appreciation, forgiveness, and love required comes only from God. He grows that fruit of His Spirit in us as we're committed to His transforming work in our lives. We simply hold out empty hands to Him to receive His grace in our lives.

Warmly,

Pamela

18
Going on a Niche Hunt

niche: a: a place, employment, or activity for which a person or thing is best fitted **b:** a habitat supplying the factors necessary for the existence of an organism or species **c:** the ecological role of an organism in a community.

All people want to feel secure and significant. We want to feel safe physically, emotionally, and relationally. We want to know we matter and that our life has meaning. We all need to find our niche. We need to know that there's a place we fit and can thrive in the community of believers called the church.

Great Expectations

Lots of people think they know what that niche is for pastors' wives. They sing, play the piano, love to teach three-year-olds in Sunday school, and attend meetings. They keep their house spick and span, lovely but without spending too much money, and always open to entertain at the drop of a suggestion. They model perfection in marriage and parenting. They're unfailingly upbeat and gracious even — or especially — when being criticized. *Et cetera. Et cetera. Ad nauseam.*

The problem with these great expectations is that we often take them seriously. Whether the pressure is external (somebody lets us know we're to be that way) or internal (we think we ought to be that way), the result is the same. We feel our security and significance means cramming ourselves into an unrealistic mold.

An Old Problem

Wondering where and how one fits his or her niche has been around at least as long ago as Moses. He was pretty confused on the whole subject.

At age 40, he acted to correct an injustice against his oppressed people. He "thought that his own people would realize that God was using him to rescue them, but they did not" (Acts 7:25).

So Moses, fleeing for his life and perhaps licking his wounds, tended sheep in the desert for 40 years. When he was 80, God told him it was time for him to fill the niche he'd been born to fill — the rescue of the Hebrews.

But the old prince-turned-shepherd resisted the idea of becoming the greatest spiritual leader in Old Testament history. He didn't think he had what it took to fill that role. "Who am I, that I should... bring the Israelites out of Egypt?" he questioned God (Exod. 3:11).

The man was full of insecurity about doing what God called him to do. The issue he seemed to stumble over most was "I have never been eloquent.... I am slow of speech and tongue"

(Exod. 4:10). In other words, Moses just *knew* that to lead he needed to be one great orator, and he didn't qualify.

Despite objections, Moses answered God's call on his life and took off to take on Pharaoh. And it was a bust. The king said, "Let your people go? No way!" Furthermore, he made the harsh life of the Israelites even more cruel with the result that they turned on Moses.

Moses wasn't surprised. It was just as he suspected — leading the Israelites wasn't his niche. He had told the Lord so before, and he told Him again (Exod. 6:12): "If the Israelites will not listen to me, why would Pharaoh listen to me, since I speak with faltering lips?"

Get it? Moses thought doing God's will — leading a couple of million people from Egypt to Canaan — depended on his way with words, and he definitely wasn't the speaker type.

Apparently he didn't need to be the speaker type because he did, indeed, guide his people to freedom.

You're Called, Right?

We can have preconceived notions of what we should be and do if God calls us to be a pastor's wife. Pastors' wives we saw as we were growing up often shape our ideas of this. (Children and adolescents are notorious for arriving at adulthood having picked up misconceptions along the way.) Maybe our notions were formed as we read books or attended workshops on "How to Be the Ideal Pastor's Wife." Perhaps they came in a dream after a bad bout of indigestion. And then there are always people who like life nice and tidy, which means they love to control others, including their pastor's wife, by defining their roles and responsibilities.

So it's not strange that when God calls us to be ministry

wives, sometimes we pull a Moses. We begin to enlighten the Omniscient by explaining how inadequate we are for the job. Then, because all jobs have a negative side and to fail is human, we can easily collect evidence that, sure enough, we're not up to the task.

If God calls us, however, then we are the right person for this place and task at this time. He's given us the gifts we need to function productively in His kingdom. He can use our personality, skills, education, and even weaknesses and inadequacies to accomplish the role in the church that is uniquely ours.

How we do our ministry may look different than we'd like, than the way our predecessor did it, or than some church members who have another job description in mind for us. So be it. And that's really OK.

When I get to heaven, God won't say, "Why weren't you more like your predecessor in this ministry? Or a better Jill Briscoe? Or a better Mother Teresa?" If He says anything of this nature at all, it will be, "Why weren't you a better Pamela Heim?"

Mission Possible

It's possible for us ministry wives to revel in our God-given gifts and talents, accept our weaknesses and inadequacies with equanimity, be content to express our unique personalities, and even feel at ease about not measuring up to some people's expectations.

To do that, however, we have to commit to some principles: 1) We live on the basis that God is the audience we want to please. We have a much higher goal than pleasing people, that is, pleasing God by loving those we serve. (If we haven't thought through the difference between loving and pleasing people, we'd better!) 3) We believe that God is pleased when we are the distinctive person, living by His Holy Spirit, that He created us to be. He's not pleased when we try to become clones or composites of Ideal Pastors' Wives. 4) We believe that God wrote His will into the core of our beings by the gifts He's given us. When we exercise our gifts in the power of the Holy Spirit, we are serving Him and His church well.

When we practice these principles, we find and fill our niche.

For Personal Meditation & Group Discussion

1. Read Exodus 3:10-4:18 and list the various objections Moses raised to God's call. Meditate on God's responses to Moses' objections. How can you apply this to yourself?

2. Consider God's call and the responses of Isaiah (6:1-8) and Jeremiah (1:4-8) when God told them the niche they were to fill. (See, you're not alone in wondering if you're up to the job!)

3. Study 1 Corinthians 12:1-11 and 1 Peter 4:10-11. Who gives spiritual gifts and for what purpose? Is it possible God has made a mistake with what He handed out to you and called you to do?

4. If you suffer the pain (maybe even paralysis) of niche comparison, what does Romans 12:3-8 and 1 Corinthians 12:14-25 say to you?

Dear Friend,

A short time ago a woman approached me saying, "Whew! That Dorothy Dahlman! She is some lady!"

It was with the utmost sincerity that I replied, "Yes, she is. And I'm profoundly grateful to Dorothy for the solid foundation she left for me to build upon in my ministry."

Dorothy formerly directed the ministry that I now lead. She retired after many years of outstanding service that positively changed the face of women's ministries in our denomination.

Then the woman continued to press her point: "Those are some shoes to fill." (Was she implying that she doubted my abilities?)

Well, I thought of my size 5 feet and mused to myself, *I don't fill most shoes I find in the store! Especially those on sale.* But I replied to my sister, who knew a good woman when she saw her, "I don't even try to fill Dorothy's shoes. I'm just trying to use the gifts God gave me to do what He's called me to do."

That's a lesson I've learned the hard way and still have to learn on occasion.

I recall a time I spoke at a big convention. Another woman was also speaking there, and she looked like something from Vogue — *perfectly* turned out, shall we say? I truly felt like a dandelion next to an orchid.

I had quite an emotional time with God, telling Him that if He had speakers like Chari, He didn't need me. Nobody needed me. Poor me. Think I'll go eat worms. Threw myself quite a pity party.

I don't know how God speaks to you, but He said something like this to me: "Pammy, you really are inadequate — that's never been the issue. The point is that I am adequate, and I gave you gifts for ministry. You have what you need to serve Me in the work I ask you to do."

As a friend used to say, "Well, shut my mouth!" Precisely. He shut my mouth.

So here I am, serving God. I speak. I write. I counsel. I teach. I lead. And gobs of women do what I do better than I do it. But the crazy-wonder of it all is this: I minister to women, and some of them have been gracious enough to tell me it's changed their lives. Amazing grace.

Warmly,

Pamela

19
Signing Up to Have an Impact

A woman bought postage stamps one day with the name and face of Clara Maas. Not knowing who Clara was, she looked for her name in an encyclopedia; it wasn't there. Later she learned that Clara Maas died of the disease for which she'd given her life to find a cure.

Reading about this, I checked my *World Book;* and though I didn't find a word about Clara, I did find information on macaroni. Wouldn't you think somebody who had a postage stamp commemorating her deserves equal billing with macaroni?

The omission of women's achievement from history and reference books can keep many of us ignorant of the significant impact we women have had on history, including church history. And make no mistake about it, women have made a difference in our world.

My deep desire is to motivate ordinary Christian women to

believe they can have a great impact on their world. One way to do this is to explore women's historical accomplishments.

Foundational to the contribution of **Mary, Mother of Jesus,** was her attitude. "Be it done to me according to your will" was her response when the angel Gabriel visited her to tell her that she was to birth the Messiah. Without consulting her parents or husband-to-be (apparently God hadn't consulted them first either), she embraced God's plan to incubate Jesus in her womb. We dare not gloss over the humiliation, confusion, and danger of her decision to obey God. She risked greatly.

Another woman had a great impact on our world because of her motherhood — **Susanna Wesley.** Of her 19 children, only nine lived to adulthood. She taught them to read and study, even writing three textbooks for them. Son John founded the Methodist church and son Charles wrote many hymns. As Susanna cared for her children, did she know she was nurturing a revival?

Bible studies met in Susanna's home in Epworth on Sunday nights, and as many as 200 people attended them. When Susanna's pastor-husband was out of town, she taught the classes. It's no wonder her son John allowed women in teaching and leadership roles in the Methodist church — he had seen the effectiveness of his mother's ministry.

In opening her home for Bible studies, Susanna was doing something Lydia did in the early church. **Lydia** met Jesus as a result of Paul's response to the Macedonian call to "Come over and help us." Lydia, owner of an elegant fabric business, may have been his first convert in Europe. Acts records that she opened her home for a house church — a center for worship, prayer, and teaching.

Lydia was simply one in a long line of women who have

used their homes as a base for ministry. Even today women are the backbone of the small group Bible study movement that results in thousands of women searching the Scriptures together.

Fabiola, who died before 200 A.D., was a well-to-do woman who served Jesus with excellence. She impressed her pagan society by her care for the sick. Some credit her with establishing the first hospital in Europe.

Fabiola was just one of a long train of Christian women who have taken care of the sick, wounded, and dying in Jesus' name. Such compassion has motivated many Christian women to become nurses and doctors. Though female physicians are rather common today, at the turn of the century they were not well received in our country. Women who wanted to serve the Lord through medicine, however, found ready acceptance in other countries. Consequently, a hundred years ago there were **100 women missionary doctors** serving in other lands. What Mother Teresa did in caring for the dying in our own time simply continued women's historical role of giving medical care for Jesus' sake.

Christian women have always been at the forefront of what we call social ministries. I think of some **Quaker women** who moved in the circles of the English aristocracy and also moved into London's prisons to protest the conditions there. When men told them to leave because the jails were not fit for ladies, they pointed out that the jails were not fit for any human being. They demanded that prisons be improved.

Sojourner Truth and **the Grimke sisters** gave leadership and money and spoke out for the causes of both abolishing slavery and gaining women the right to vote, issues they supported from Scripture. Also it was women who began the

Women's Christian Temperance Union to combat the evils of alcoholism and its destruction of family life. Maybe it's not surprising then that a modern woman started Mothers Against Drunk Drivers (MADD) to combat vehicular murder on America's highways.

Catherine Booth was wife of William Booth, mother of eight children and cofounder of the Salvation Army. After the birth of her fourth child, Catherine felt called to preach. (Some say she preached better than her husband. She said she felt as comfortable in the pulpit as in her kitchen.) She also worked with rehabilitating prostitutes in London, a ministry that helped form the foundation of the Army's famous social action ministries. Her daughter **Evangeline** became the head of the Salvation Army in the United States when she was 31 years old and later was named general of the Salvation Army worldwide. (An interesting footnote is that each married Booth daughter retained her maiden name, hypenating Booth with her husband's last name. And we think that's new-fangled!)

Twenty years after Catherine Booth's birth, **Mary Slessor** was born to an alcoholic father and a mother who worked long days in a factory. Mary was one of seven children, and those kids played missionary the way kids play house. Mother Slessor hoped one of her sons would go to Africa as a missionary, but all the sons died young. Mary, however, got to Africa and served Christ and His church there. She spread the gospel, rescued hundreds of babies from death, and ended up being the first woman named a vice consul of the British Empire.

Speaking of **women missionaries**, by 1830, 49 percent of all missionaries were women, and by 1880, 57 percent of all missionaries were women. By 1929, that figure went up to 67 percent — *more than two-thirds of the whole missionary force at* *that time were women.*

We owe women **songwriters and authors** a debt every time we sing "Just As I Am," "Like a River Glorious," and "Be Still, My Soul." Our church hymnbooks would be poorer without the contributions of women like Frances Ridley Havergal and Fanny Crosby. Likewise, a look at our Christian libraries reveals how much richer our spiritual lives are because of the writings of devout and gifted women.

Isabella Graham and Joanna Graham Bethune organized the first society for promoting Sunday schools in America. Sunday schools back then educated children who labored six long days a week and didn't get to school. Sunday school taught those poor children how to read, using the Bible as a text.

I could go on but time would fail me to tell of Marcella and Monica, Katie Luther and Catherine Bannister, Phoebe Palmer and Phoebe Yoder. "Others, refusing to accept freedom, died under torture in order to be raised to a better life. Some were mocked and whipped, and others were put in chains and taken off to prison. They were stoned, they were sawn in two, they were killed by the sword.... The world was not good enough for them!... What a record all of these have won by their faith" (Heb. 11:35-39 TEV).

My observations in this country and some others convinces me that godly women continue to be the backbone of paid and volunteer ministries. Take the ministries of Christian women and the services of secular women away, and our world would be in an enormously larger mess than it is. In developing countries I've visited, I've seen women doing hard, dirty, dangerous ministries to the glory of God and the advancement of His gospel.

Let's not miss the fact that heroes of the faith consistently consider themselves ordinary women. They are rich and poor, married and single, educated and uneducated, homemakers and professional women. The majority have received little status in the world's eyes, and they haven't been important in their own.

So how did and do they make such a difference? These ordinary women have an extraordinary God, and they are dead earnest about being faithful to His call and moving out into the world to express His love.

I pray that you, I, and all other ordinary Christian women will catch a glimpse of our potential to make a difference in our world, embrace and fully use our gifts to build the church, and risk being as effective and useful as God can make us. A cloud of witnesses in God's Hall of Faithful Women stands on the sidelines cheering us on! We can be and do all God wants us to be and do. I know we can.

We must if Aburdene and Naisbitt are right that "When it comes to 'saving the world,' or a part of it, street by street, neighborhood by neighborhood, women are the catalysts through whom the critical mass for social change will be achieved" (*Megatrends for Women*, p. 265).

For Personal Meditation & Group Discussion

1. If you could do one thing for people in general or women in particular, what would it be? Do you consider that your ministry passion? If not, what is your passion?

2. Do you have a sense of God's call on your life? If so, what is it? How did you come to that conclusion?

3. What are your spiritual gifts? Your skills? What limits your developing them and using them fully for Jesus' sake?

4. When you get to heaven, what do you think Jesus will ask concerning your call, gifts, and ministries? How will you be able to respond?

Dear Friend,

One aspect of revitalizing a church or ministry is to research its history. To build for the future, it needs to understand its past.

I think women who follow Jesus need to know their great heritage and history. A couple of years ago I developed a message series, "Jesus Cares for Women," and began to share it at retreats. Invariably, women would come up to me after I'd spoken and say something like this, "I'd never before understood how radical Jesus was in His positive treatment of women or how much respect and love He gave them."

Talking with Christians, I could easily get the impression that the issue of the role of women in the church is a modern one foisted on it by the feminist movement in the past 35 years. Many women have only the vaguest idea about the accomplishments of their sisters throughout church history and their significant part in building the kingdom.

As I write this, it's summer. I've had time to do considerable thinking about my purpose in ministry. It boils down to this: I want women to be and do all that God created and called them to be and do. And make no mistake about it, I'm passionate about this. It excites, motivates, drives, and energizes me.

It sobers me as well, for I look at a church made up of more women than men and see a majority of that majority content to do their little bit for Jesus while the world is dying for need of the Savior. I see in too many daughters of the Almighty One a sense of hopelessness and helplessness in the face of persistent problems and prevalent evil. I see too many followers of the

All-sufficient One too focused on their inadequacy to embrace opportunities for ministry. I see too much doubt that crushes trust, too much fear that drowns courage, and too great an attachment to comfort and convenience that refuses to risk.

And the worst part is, I see this in myself and do mighty battle with it all the time. I'm Moses yammering that God should find somebody else for the job. I'm Isaiah trying to sideline myself because of unworthiness. I'm Jeremiah pointing out my incompetence. I'm Peter coming up with "biblical" reasons why I can't go to whom God sends me. I'm just Pamela saying I'm too busy, too tired, and too little. I'm also Mary embracing God's will for me and struggling to understand it when the way gets rough. Underneath it all, my passion is to be and do what God wants me to be and do.

The women you read about in this chapter had that same desire. They were weak, flawed, needy, and sinful like me, but they persevered to answer God's call on their lives. Will you join me in doing the same?

Warmly,

Pamela

20

The Gift of a Second Chance

The story is familiar. When God called Jonah to minister in Nineveh, Jonah consulted with his travel agent, heard a ship headed for Tarshish was in port, and booked passage. A storm came up, and Jonah landed in the drink, where a big fish swallowed him. Somewhere in the fish's digestive system, Jonah held a prayer meeting. It turned out Jonah caused severe indigestion, so the fish threw him up on dry land. Then God recommissioned him, and this time the reluctant prophet walked Nineveh's streets declaring impending doom. The people repented, God relented, and Jonah's nose got badly out of joint as a result.

For us women who serve God, this story is wonderfully encouraging on at least four counts.

About Ordinary Ornery People

The book of Jonah is an unflattering account of a disobedient, narrow-minded, pouting kind of guy. When at the end of the story I picture him sitting under a dead vine and whining that he wants to die, I'd like to shake him. I may be in heaven several centuries before I get motivated to look up old Jonah.

Still, Jonah reminds you and me that an ordinary, ornery person can have a huge influence. Jonah's reluctant preaching brought a whole city to repentance.

Today Christian women desperately need a renewed vision of the positive impact one life can make. Every one of us can confidently embrace the tasks God gives us to do, certain that He can use even us.

That means we'll need to stop focusing on our limits. God told me a long time ago that my problem isn't that I *feel* inadequate—I really *am* inadequate. I'm not good enough, smart enough, strong enough in any way to minister fruitfully. Despite this insufficiency, each of us has a task to do that no other person can do in just the way we can do it. So, though we are common, ordinary, and sometimes even ornery people, we have an uncommon, extraordinary God who chooses to use people like us to build His kingdom.

About Open Doors

The story of Jonah reminds us that circumstances dovetailed nicely to enable the prophet to run away from God's will. When he chose to rebel by going to Tarshish instead of Nineveh, a ship happened to be in port, it happened to have room for him, and he happened to have fare for the journey.

One of the most harmful myths in American Christianity is that God's will should make our lives smooth and uncomplicated. I've heard people say they must be out of God's will because things are difficult for them.

To these people, I've wanted to say (and sometimes have), "What about Mary, the mother of Jesus?" She was in God's will, yet she was inconvenienced, ostracized, and heartbroken despite the fact she was within God's will in delivering His Son into a world that murdered Him.

Open doors and smooth circumstances don't necessarily indicate we're in God's will. In fact, we can be doing exactly what God has called us to do and find doors slamming in our faces. If we don't understand that serving God may be no easier for us than it was for Mary, we could easily fall into the trap of disobedient Jonah, walking though doors swinging on well-greased hinges. Doors that may lead out on the broad and smooth path of destruction, when our intent is to stay put on the narrow and sometimes rough trail of God's will.

About Staying in God's Will

While we can choose the easy road and disobey God, I don't think it's all that simple to walk away from Him.

I once thought missing God's will for my life was the easiest thing in the world. As a kid and young adult, I worried that somehow inadvertently, even unconsciously, I would take a wrong step.

Jonah shows us that taking a 180-degree turn from God's will usually requires a deliberate, volitional act; and even then God doesn't let go of us quickly or easily. As the poet Francis Thompson penned, God is the hound of heaven who doesn't stop pursuing His children even when they run from Him.

Believing it's difficult to escape God may cause one of two feelings. We may feel frustrated or even frightened if we don't trust and value the "Love that wilt not let me go." But if we treasure the tenacious tenderness of Jesus, we will find great security in knowing God keeps on extending opportunities to repent after we've blown it.

If Jonah couldn't get away from God even when he wanted to, how much harder it is to miss God's will when we deeply and truly yearn to have a solid, satisfying relationship with Him.

About Second Chances

Psychologist Sandra Wilson once said her favorite Bible verse is Jonah 3:1. *"The word of God came a second time to Jonah."*

As a kid I heard if at any point I disobeyed God's will, I would never find my way back to it. I'd forever have to settle for what preachers and Sunday school teachers called "God's second best."

Others must have heard this, too, because I run into lots of Christians who serve a God with a short fuse, a quick temper, and a long memory. He's a touchy, irritable Parent who can't wait to write His children out of His will.

Jonah, however, was right when He reminded God in prayer that He is slow to anger and long-suffering. Jonah could read in Israel's history proof of God's patience. When I read the history of God's people in the Old Testament, I know I'd have run out of forbearance and disciplined them long before God ever did. So it wasn't out of character for God to give Jonah a second chance — just as He later gave Peter and John Mark another chance.

While this is true, we realize we can make decisions we can never undo, and we'll live with the consequences of our bad choices for the rest of our lives. Having said this, however, the truth remains that there's nothing God cannot forgive. Nothing He can't redeem. Nothing He can't transform and work together for our good as Romans 8:28 promises. That's because God's grace is infinitely great — greater than all our finite sins. The gospel, as Jonah shows us, is the good news of second — third and fourth — chances.

One Final Thought

The Scottish minister, Alexander Whyte, once described the perseverance of the saints as falling down and getting up, falling down and getting up, falling down and getting up the whole way to heaven.

Had there been a fifth chapter of Jonah, I'd like to think it would have said something like this: "Jonah felt remorse for wishing the death of 120,000 little Ninevite children. His repentance led him to value Ninevites because God did." In my expanded version of Jonah, the man — who had fallen down and gotten up only to fall down again — reached out one more time and took God's hand and kept on walking toward heaven in obedient service to God and others despite his own constant inadequacies and frequent failures along the way.

For this new decade and century and all the time left to us women in ministry, I pray that we will be and do all God calls us to be and do, that we'll not get easily discouraged by closed doors, that we'll seize the opportunities of second chances. I pray we'll get up when we fall down, keep walking toward heaven, and continue to be obedient to our calling to service.

For Personal Meditation & Group Discussion

1. What lesson from Jonah most encourages you in your current situation?

2. Read Matthew 26:69-74. What was Peter's sin? Have you ever been so betrayed by a friend? How serious an offense would you call that? Then ponder Mark 16:1-7. Of all the disciples, why do you think Jesus specifically mentioned Peter? Now look at John 21:15-17. What did this conversation mean in terms of second chances?

3. We know that Judas betrayed Jesus. How do you think Jesus might have responded to Judas after the resurrection if Judas had not committed suicide? Why do you think that? (For a fun, creative exercise, try writing a different, more positive end to the life of Judas.)

4. God sometimes expresses His willingness to give second chances through others. Read and reflect on Acts 15:37-40. What did the young man do with his second chance? (Clues: Read 2 Timothy 4:11 and also consider the title of the second Gospel.)

5. Did/do you ever wrestle with the idea that you've blown it so often or so badly that God has demoted or disowned you? Where did you get the idea that God rejects you if you fail?

6. Would you say you generally react like Paul or Barnabas when those with whom you serve fail? (Consider the possibility that your answer may be related to your answers to #5.)

Dear Friend,

Where did I get the idea that the older I got, the easier I'd find the life of faith? I *know* I had my life put together better in my 20s, 30s, and 40s than I have now in my 50s.

I talk to many women who report the same thing. They lament that faith felt so much more simple yesterday than it does today. They didn't used to realize just how weak and wounded and needy and sinful they've discovered themselves to be. They see themselves thinking, feeling, and behaving in ways that don't fit with their old ideas of godliness.

They wonder, do real saints have as many doubts as I've come to have? After years of being nice, do truly mature Christians find that their anger seems to simmer more frequently? Do they feel tired to the point of wanting to run away from the unresolved problems that continue unresolved? Do they feel disappointed with life and, thus, with God? Having fallen short of her own high standard, does a really good Christian ever feel that it would be easier just to give up trying one more time?

Back in the 1970s, a catchy statement was often repeated: "Please be patient with me. God isn't finished with me yet." The appeal was to give time and space to others as they pursued growth in grace and truth.

I've come to realize that more and more I'm saying as I counsel women, "Please be patient with yourself. God isn't finished with you yet" — though perhaps not in those very words. I observe so much impatience within women because of their sense of inadequacy in ministry, because of the pain of their particular thorn in the flesh that they think they ought to be able to remove through prayer and trust, because of their besetting sins over which they've yet to gain victory, or because of their deep reluctance to move out of their comfort zones to follow God's call.

Undoubtedly there's a strong streak of perfectionism in us all, and impatience to boot. We want to be flawless and we want it now. The good news is that Jesus already sees us that way. Hebrews 10:14 defines the paradox of the already-but-not-yet nature of our perfection: Jesus has made us perfect (already) forever while He's still making us holy (in process).

I love new things. I love the start of a new month or a new year. I like anything that symbolizes the possibility of turning over a new leaf, making a fresh start, initiating needed changes. That's why the story of Jonah provides solid encouragement. I thought you might like to reflect on the grace of second chances along with me.

Warmly,

Pamela

21

Close (Staff) Encounters of the Complex Kind

At my husband's company picnic, a woman told me about a visit she'd had with her sister. She described a sibling who acted rigidly and insensitively. She said, "The more I'm around her, the less I like her."

I replied, "What I hear you saying is that sometimes we're related to people we'd never choose as friends."

I'm the oldest of five children in a family. I know all five of us have the same parents, so it puzzles me how we can each be so different. Certain siblings seem to have more natural affinity with each other than they do with the rest of us, and a couple seem to rub each other the wrong way fairly consistently.

I've also seen how mothers can wrestle with liking one

child's spouse and feeling barely civil to another son- or daughter-in-law.

Does any of this resonate with what you've discovered about families created by both biology and marriage?

The Staff Family

I thought about this when I pondered the subject of what is called the staff family, that group of people who work together to serve a local church. The typical perception is that this group of people will like each other, get along well together, and feel a sense of emotional closeness with each other. In short, they will be like family to one another.

Ah, that is exactly what the reality may be! Like biological families, members of a staff family are sometimes (more often than we'd like to think?) very different from each other. Sometimes their personalities may even rub each other the wrong way to such an extent that friction is apparent. They may be a staff family, but they're not close and cherished friends.

But We're All Christians!

For some reason, however, that disturbs our sense of rightness. We think it shouldn't be that way. Surely, since we're all Christians, we ought to enjoy each other, shouldn't we? Well, maybe, if being a Christ-follower means we're all exactly alike and have achieved perfection. But we're imperfect and as unique as our fingerprints.

Even a woman in a wonderful marriage has to deal with barriers to intimacy with her husband, and she chose to marry that man. So is it any wonder that a staff team experiences difficulties? And you dated your husband longer and with more intense scrutiny (I hope!) than you "courted" the staff whom you joined or who joined you. In fact, staff often come together in an "arranged marriage" in which you had no decision at all. Though we know all this intellectually, it's still tough to deal emotionally with the reality that a staff family doesn't give us what we naturally and desperately yearn for, what Anne of Green Gables called a "bosom friend." To realize other staff wives are more coworkers than nurturing family members or best friends can be a tremendous disappointment.

The Ingredients of Friendship

What could make another staff wife or woman on the church staff be your friend and not simply a colaborer in ministry? Let's consider some of the ingredients of friendship, the "least natural of loves" according to C. S. Lewis.

Commonality. Friendship is based on having things in common with another. That may be similarity in age, past and present experiences, interests and hobbies, likes and dislikes, sense of humor, values and priorities, temperament, or outlook on life. On the contrary, it's hard to be friends with one with whom you have little in common.

Commitment. Friends have an agreement with each other whether spoken or not. They are committed to being vulnerable, honest, and loyal to each other. Friends self-disclose. They know, without saying, that their personal communication is privileged information, and they keep confidences.

Acceptance. Friends give each other acceptance. They recognize each other's weaknesses and celebrate strengths. They skillfully treasure the grain and graciously blow the chaff away.

Respect. For all their commonality, friends respect differences. Each respects the individuality of the other. Each respects the boundaries of the other. They give each other space when needed.

Chemistry: This is an illusive quality, but friends experience a mutual liking that they often can't explain. "We just hit it off!" they'll say.

With all this in mind, it's obvious that just because two persons happen to be in the same place at the same time for the same purpose doesn't necessarily mean they will be great friends. So how do you live and work amiably with staff wives you wouldn't normally choose as friends?

For the Senior Pastor's Wife

Like it or not, being the senior pastor's wife puts you in a different role than other staff wives. Others look to you for direction. They may consider you their example. That's an awesome privilege as well as responsibility. What you may want to model for them is how to grow in your own spiritual life, how to be a supportive wife without losing your individuality, how to make choices based on God's will rather than others' demands, how to be thoughtful and kind, how to be hospitable, how to control your tongue, how to deal with personal conflicts. The point is, if before God you're modeling progress, not perfection — becoming (even if slowly!) the woman God wants you to be — that's the best you can do for them.

Second, if you want to have influence and impact with others, you'll have to foster some level of connection with them. Some staff wives and women may find an occasional note, card, or phone call enough to satisfy their need for connection with you. If a ministry relationship is rocky, you may find, as I do, that it helps to choose deliberately to spend more time with the person whom you find difficult.

Third, use your spiritual gifts to benefit your staff family as well as the larger church body. If teaching, gather staff women together for occasional Bible studies. If it's administration, delegate some aspect of nurturing staff wives' relationships to a staff wife who has gifts that encourage group fellowship. For example, you may not have a gift of hospitality, but another wife does. Ask her to work with you to develop get-togethers for the group. (Notice, working alongside her indicates that she needs your partnership and support in this.) If it's mercy, be on the lookout for ways to encourage staff wives when they're going through hard times. You get the idea.

Fourth, consider getting all the staff wives together to read this book. Then discuss your responses to the issues raised in it.

For All Ministry Women

Every ministry wife needs to trust God that she is linked to these staff people in this situation for a divine purpose. Consider the possibility that you may need to have some of the rough edges sanded from your personality. These relationships may point out areas for your spiritual and emotional growth. Be humble enough to learn what you can.

Second, give yourself permission to relate to staff women and wives as coworkers and beloved members of the body of Christ rather than as best friends. Refuse false guilt about this — don't "should" on yourself. You have the right to choose your best friends. You have the right to choose how much time you can devote to any one staff woman or wife. (This permission keeps you from getting swallowed by the neediness of a person who wants more than you can reasonably give.) Likewise, confront unrealistic expectations you may have of others. Ask yourself, "Is it reasonable for me to expect this person to treat me as her best friend?"

Third, though you may not necessarily have enough

common ground for a nurturing friendship, value whatever is good and healthy in the your relationships with colleagues.

Fourth, if you sense tension in a relationship with another staff wife or woman, don't simply hope it will go away. Take the initiative to go to the woman and say, "I sense there's some tension between us. Have I offended you in any way? Can we talk about this? I do want to be a friend."

Fifth, practice forbearance and forgiveness. Anytime people live and work together, annoyances and misunderstandings are bound to happen. Patience and granting pardon are traits of authentic Christianity.

In all that you do as a team working for the same purpose, pray to model relationships in such as way that the church can say, "My, how they love one another."

STAFF RELATIONSHIP FACTS

Hurt people hurt people. Family dysfunction in our society means there's a high probability that church staffs will include bruised individuals. Some people have significant pathologies that make for chaotic relationships. Understanding that some people — even in Christian ministry — have wounded souls resulting in significant dysfunction can set you free from feeling you're crazy or bad because you can't fix the distressing relationship. Personality disorders, frankly, require intentional, professional treatment just as do illnesses of the body.

Common characteristics of wounded and wounding people are:

1) They often see things in extremes — black and white, good and bad. They may be rigid and legalistic.
2) They often have a strong need to control.
3) They may see disagreements as win-lose, not win-win, situations, and they have to win.
4) They grew up with chaos; therefore they may create the familiarity of turmoil.
5) Because of early emotional deficits, they can't get enough affirmation and love. They can exhaust you with their demands for attention, help, and recognition.
6) They're usually oblivious to their problems and those they create for others.
7) You can feel crazy around them — like you're missing something or losing it — though you feel sane around others.

For Personal Meditation & Group Discussion

1. Jesus colabored with 12 apostles, but He included just Peter, James, and John in His inner circle. What does it mean to you that nine were not in that intimate group? Do you give yourself freedom to choose the degree of closeness you have with staff members? Give them freedom to choose how they want to relate to you?

2. According to "one another" passages such as John 13:34, 1 Thessalonians 5:11, Colossians 3:9, James 5:16, Galatians 5:13, and Ephesians 4:32, how are you to relate to colleagues? What are the principles? Consider how do you apply them with people who aren't "bosom friends"?

3. What does 1 Corinthians 13 say to you about acting with love toward people — enemies or close friends? How can you show love to colleagues you don't naturally like?

4. Paul and Barnabas disagreed and separated as a result (Acts 15:36-41), and God gave both of them fruit in subsequent ministries. Are disagreements between ministry colleagues always about who's right and wrong? Do you have or give yourself permission to disagree agreeably in your team? Why or why not?

5. Since you can't fix others, only yourself, do you have personal issues (need for approval or to control, unhealthy competitiveness, fear of failure or abandonment, pride, codependency) that hamper relationships with your staff family? If so, ask God for help and healing in that area. If you feel stuck on an issue, seek out healing resources to use.

Dear Friend,

I met with a group of pastors' wives a while back. I always treasure such times of connecting in person.

I asked this question: What didn't you know about being a pastor's wife that you wish you had known before becoming one? I got many responses.

- I wish I'd have known not to wait for people to step up and volunteer since that won't happen. I wish I'd have known the importance of communicating the need and how to recruit people to be involved in meeting it.
- I wish I'd have known there's no one right way to be a pastor's wife, that there's no one mold that I have to fit.
- I wish I'd have known more about dealing with expectations about my children. My expectations for them got me into trouble though my heart was in the right place — I wanted to protect them from being criticized by people in the church. I'm glad my husband had a better perspective on this than I did.
- I wish I'd have known how hard it is to work on staff relationships. I'm guessing that in no other profession do the wives expect to be compatible to the degree pastors' wives expect themselves to be.

In these statements I heard real women in real situations indicate that they have learned real truth and made real progress in applying it. In the last statement, I heard an idea for this chapter. As I've spoken with pastors' wives in several settings, I've heard concern, frustration, and pain about staff

Close (Staff) Encounters of the Complex Kind / 235

relationships.

Perhaps you're a lone pastor's wife in a church where your husband is the whole staff. I hope you'll find some of the principles discussed in this issue applicable to other relationships in which you may find yourself. Or maybe you can tuck away these thoughts for another day when you'll be part of a multiple-staff church.

Warmly,

Pamela

Part 5

Relating to Others: Wise as Serpent, Harmless as Dove

22

An Interview on Friendship

I asked five pastors' wives — Gayle, Cindy, Joyce, Kathryn, and Kristine — to share their insights on friendship with other ministry wives. I think they'll give you food for thought.

PHH: Some say a pastor's wife can't have good friends — especially not in her husband's congregation. What do you say?

Cindy: I say a pastor's wife without good friends is on the way to a nervous breakdown or worse! Jesus had 12 good friends and three among those who were kindred spirits. Following His example is pretty wise.

Kathryn: A person to have fun with and vent with is essential to handling the pressures of church life. A pastor's wife *must* have good friends — some inside and some outside the congregation.

Cindy: I've had close friends in and out of both churches we've served. My emotional health and spiritual growth is too important to sacrifice friendship out of concern someone might feel jealous.

Gayle: I've found it easier at times to have my best friends outside of the church. I've had friends within the church, and it's worked because the woman was a mature, growing Christian. Most people were unaware of the time we spent together outside the church.

Kathryn: My church friends are careful not to monopolize my attention in the foyer on Sunday, and I'm accessible to others.

Joyce: I'm careful not to be exclusive, so if someone feels less loved by me than they think they deserve, then that is their problem. I refuse to feel guilty.

Kristine: Church women *need* to see healthy models of women's friendships in and out of church.

PHH: How did you go about finding a trusted friend with whom you can be honest and show your weaknesses?

Joyce: I pray to God to bring that friend along. As she opens the friendship door, I say, "Thank You, Lord."

Kristine: I talked to everybody — in the grocery store, at church, at the children's school, at other churches' Bible studies. Eventually I narrowed it down to about five people to call on. I verbalized my desire to make friends with these women who seemed to be of a kindred spirit. A couple seemed surprised and then flattered! It was the beginning of a great bond.

Gayle: I've looked for women who have been involved or are in the ministry — missionaries, others pastors' wives in the area, or wives of men who used to be in the ministry.

Cindy: I've found my close friendships among those with

whom I'm involved in ministry. Most of the time we're in the same life stage, but not always.

Kathryn: I was very lonely the first year at this church. Gradually I learned which women shared my interests and which could be trusted. Also, my best friendships were formed out of the prayer groups in which I've participated, especially a prayer group of other pastors' wives with whom I've met every Saturday morning.

PHH: What makes your friendships meaningful?

Kathryn: In my pastors' wives group, we've usually been more honest with each other than we are with our husbands — and we've held each other accountable. These women have loved me through the difficulties and helped me deal constructively with areas in which God wants me to grow. With them I've found fellowship, nurture, counsel, exhortation, and corporate worship. We share common interests, but we're not exactly alike.

Cindy: We serve, pray, laugh, and cry together and encourage each other.

Kristine: My friends and I look for ways to be together for fun — we laugh together as often as possible! We pray for each other weekly and keep each other's spirits up.

Joyce: A friendship is meaningful to me if the person is one I can relax, laugh, and pray with. We share similar interests and help each other with tasks that frustrate us.

Gayle: I'd say it's sharing spiritual things as well as personal concerns.

PHH: But are there limits to what a pastor's wife may share with a friend?

Gayle: Very personal things about your marriage are probably not appropriate. However, I do feel comfortable sharing more of those kinds of things if the woman is not a member of our congregation. A trusted friend still likes and respects my husband even if I complain a little about him.

Kristine: I believe there are different limits with each friend. Some of my friends are better suited than others for listening and confiding in — for instance, marriage problems. I confide little bits at a time to see whom I can trust.

Cindy: I believe that we don't share family conflict without the family's permission. Also, in the course of ministry I hear things that have been shared in confidence, and this confidence must always be honored by not sharing it with anybody else.

Kathryn: I don't share confidences concerning a third party with my friend, nor do I say things about my husband that would cast him in a bad light, particularly if the friend is within the church.

Joyce: I should not share anything if my husband's or any other individual's privacy is violated by my talking about it. Christ is my best friend, and I share with Him what I should not share with others.

PHH: Has your trust ever been betrayed by a friend? If so, how did you handle that? And did you find it hard to trust again?

Gayle: That hasn't happened to me.

Kristine: Nor to me.

Joyce: I was burned as a child by girlfriends and felt angry and hurt. I learned then that only Christ is my perfect friend at times like those. I've found it helpful to write poetry and journal my thoughts as prayers.

Kathryn: I've not been betrayed by a good friend, but I have been hurt by acquaintances who have not respected deep things I've shared in a prayer group. My response has been to guard what I say around those people.

Cindy: I've only been betrayed by a real estate agent who went to our church. I now like to keep business and financial things private and not have members of the congregation in on them.

PHH: Pastors' wives move a lot. Have you ever felt reluctant to form close friendships to avoid the pain of loss when you relocate?

Cindy: I try to live in each place as if I will be there until heaven.

Kathryn: Moving has been a hard thing for me to accept; but after several moves, I've learned that God does provide new relationships in the new place. Also I've found that He is the glue in the old friendship, holding us together though we don't see each other.

Kristine: Through trial and error I've learned that it's better to have many acquaintances for a time than to be lonely for any time!

Gayle: I've decided if I don't jump in each time, I will never have a good friend.

Joyce: Tomorrow is not a given, so I go for the friendship now because I need a friend now. With modern travel and communication, I continue meaningful friendships.

PHH: What about maintaining friendships after a move? What do you do to nurture them?

Gayle: Some friendships are definitely worth the time and effort to maintain. I have a good friend in Cameroon to whom I write each week and send pictures, videos, and the like.

Cindy: Some friendships are just for a time, but some last for a lifetime through phone calls, letters, and visits.

Kathryn: I keep in touch with old friends by writing, calling, and making an effort to get together when I'm within driving distance. Often I've found that after a few minutes of being back together, my friends and I are close again, though we haven't seen each other in months or years. I think that is a distinctive of a deep friendship. Knowing this helps me be less stressed about not writing or calling enough.

Kristine: Time and distance do test a friendship. It takes both people to keep the friendship alive. I found it helpful to talk with my friend, before I moved, about how that would change our relationship and what our expectations are about letters and the like. Also, it's important not to measure how much the other makes an effort, but to assume we're close friends and act caring.

Joyce: Friendships are eternal. I grieved leaving a dear friend months before a move we made. We now call, write, and even vacation together twice a year. We meet halfway and motel it. Our children swim while we talk, play games, and feed our souls on friendship.

PHH: What have been the positives and negatives of your relationship with your trusted friends?

Joyce: They understand, and when they don't understand they love me for myself — even if I'm not at my best. They are loving, caring people I can be real around. I don't need to play a role.

Kathryn: The positive is having someone understand me when I don't understand myself, having fun, sharing ideas and activities, being myself, and learning from my friend's insight about God and life in general. The negative is the pain of separation and sometimes not having the time to do what your friend asks.

Cindy: With two special friends at a former church, the negative was that their husbands and mine weren't buddies and were sometimes in disagreement. We women just worked around it!

Gayle: The negative for me is that I seem to choose women who also move — like pastors' wives and missionaries. On the other hand, there are a lot of interesting places I could visit!

For Personal Meditation & Group Discussion

1. Read and reflect on Job 16:20; Psalm 119:63; Proverbs 17:17, 18:24, 22:11, 27:6, 27:9-10; Ecclesiastes 4:10; and John 15:13-15. What do these verses tell you about friendship?

2. If you have some "good enough" friends, list some ways you might strengthen your relationship with them. Share them with another person who can hold you accountable.

3. Consider contacting an old friend with whom you may have lost touch. Who would that be? Why would reconnecting with her be pleasant for you? What would keep you from doing this?

4. If you don't have a safe friend, ask God to give you one or two good friends who will be channels of His love. Pray with a prayer partner about this.

5. How comfortable do you feel being *totally* honest with God about all that you're thinking and feeling? Have you ever written a letter to Jesus when you're distressed by something you feel you simply can't share with another? If so, how did you find that exercise? If you've never written a letter to Jesus, what would keep you from doing so?

6. Read Dee Brestin's *The Friendships of Women,* and share what you learned from it. Or ask other women to join you in reading it, and then invite them for coffee to discuss insights you've gained.

Dear Friend,

Every time I have an opportunity to interact with large or small groups of pastors' wives, I become more and more aware that one of the issues of greatest concern to ministry women centers on friendship.

Loneliness is a most painful human emotion.

I'm not talking about being alone, because I often relish solitude to read, meditate, pray, journal, and simply renew my soul.

But I hate loneliness. I dislike that uneasy, aching feeling of being alone in places and situations where I want somebody with me. I hurt when nobody else seems to think or feel as I do. I get sad when nobody is there to listen to me or — worse yet — when somebody listens but doesn't seem to understand or care.

I believe all of us feel the need for deeply fulfilling relationships. We crave a comfortable sense of being respected, emotionally supported, and loved by people we value. We yearn to be seen and known, and not have others abandon us when they see and know us as we really are.

Adam and Eve in the Garden of Eden experienced such intimacy in a perfect relationship with each other as well as with God. But because of sin, you and I will never know that on earth. Still, we long for the intimate relationships for which we were created, and we resist loneliness.

In more than five decades, I've had numerous acquaintances, many friends, some good friends, and a couple of great friends. Despite this, as Gail Sheehy wrote in her book *Passages*,

I've experienced that "We stand alone. We are the only ones with our own set of thoughts and bundle of feelings. Another person can taste them, through shared experience or conversation, but no other person can ever really *digest* them." Our uniqueness, as well as our fear of vulnerability, is at the root of most of our loneliness.

There are no perfect relationships this side of heaven. None of us will ever find or be the ideal friend. As a result, until we die we shall feel lonely from time to time.

That occasional loneliness, however, doesn't get me down the way it once did. I've come to see that the intimacy I need most is intimacy with God. As Pascal said, the greatest vacuum in our souls is God-shaped.

A loving, communicating Creator made us to connect with Him on a deeply personal, fulfilling level. Though people can't provide us with perfect love, total acceptance, and complete respect, God can and does. He can meet our deepest longing for intimacy because He knows and loves us, and He allows us to know Him personally.

For a long time now, loneliness has been my impetus to reach out to God. What physical hunger is to eating and physical thirst is to drinking, loneliness — my soul's hunger and thirst — is to nurturing my relationship with my Friend Jesus.

I've found comfort in knowing that Jesus is always awake in the middle of the night when I want to talk. He's never too tired to listen to me. He always understands exactly how I feel. He is accurately empathic. He doesn't gossip. He doesn't stop loving me because of who I am. And when I move, He moves also. He's the perfect friend.

In saying this, I'm in no way minimizing human friendships as superfluous or saying that spiritually mature Christians don't need others. The desire you and I have for soul friends is a healthy response to the way God made us. Since I'm made for relationships, I'm grateful that Jesus has often sent His love for me through other friends of His who have offered me a listening ear, a shoulder to cry on, a pat on the back and, when I've needed it, a kick in the pants.

I want to delight in the best that human relationships have to offer me, but not demand of them more than they are capable of bringing into my life. I don't want to deal in unrealistic expectations.

Though God made us for loving relationships, no mortal can be to us what only God can be. God shaped an emptiness within us that only He can fill. You and I will experience wholeness only to the extent that we find a delightful, restful, satisfying connection with our God. To the extent that we have this, we can appreciate all the good things earthly friends bring into our lives and not weight them down with unreasonable demands.

Warmly,

23
10 Friendship Facts

We human beings have "an inexhaustible need to be loved, and a continual fear of not being loved. Constantly... we look for proofs of love.... We look for them as remedies for our solitude," wrote Swiss psychiatrist Paul Tournier.

This desire for love and community is a part of God's design. In fact, loneliness was the first thing in His new creation that God called "not good."

While we need significant relationships and long for friendships, a safe intimacy with other people doesn't happen as often or to the degree many of us wish. In focus groups across the country I've asked women about their needs, and consistently the greatest response has to do with having a truly good friend. With that in mind, I share ten friendship principles — maybe not new stuff, but important to review and digest.

1. Friendships require intentionality. Though I sometimes say what I'll buy when I win the lottery, it won't ever happen because I don't play the lottery. Never buy a ticket. Can't possibly win. By the same token, wishing doesn't create friendships.

Making and keeping friends requires personal investment. Friendships take time and energy and don't always fit conveniently into our to-do lists. People unwilling to take time to be with and be there for friends can't expect to have any. Solid friendships don't just happen.

2. Friendships are never better than the two people involved in them. In relationships, two halves don't seem to make one whole. If I'm half healthy and my friend is half healthy, our friendship will be half healthy. In relationship math, $1/2 + 1/2 = 1/2$. As individuals, we'll never feel complete with another if we're not significantly content within ourselves and in our relationship to God.

Women who look for another person to rescue, fix, or save them will drive friends away — except friends as codependent as themselves. In such a scenario, two emotionally and psychologically immature or wounded people are hoping for a healthy, satisfying friendship. It doesn't work that way.

So we have to ask ourselves, Am I my own best friend first of all? Am I the kind of healthy person I'd want as a best friend?

3. Friendships tend to be healthier if they develop step-by-step over a reasonable length of time. I recommend what I call the friendship dance. All friendships begin with an exchange of superficial information: our names, where we live, and family status. From this beginning comes the potential to end up with a significant relationship.

After dancing at the surface for a bit, one person risks revealing something about an inch deeper. She waits to see how that information is received and whether or not the other person will reciprocate by sharing more of herself. The relationship deepens in small steps as each ventures increasing self-disclosure. The risk in all this, of course, is rejection.

Sometimes a woman takes a steep dive revealing something *really big* about herself much too early into the relationship. Sometimes she expects the other to be equally intimate in her sharing and labels the other as unfriendly, cold, and guarded if she doesn't take such a plunge. In reality, the other woman who refuses to expose more of her soul is being wisely cautious until she concludes it's safe to confide at that depth.

The dance of revealing more of self and receiving understanding and acceptance with each revelation continues until one or both choose not to disclose more. Perhaps one feels judged somewhere along the line, so she feels the need to protect herself against further condemnation. If the dance may end there, the relationship plateaus or declines. Or maybe the barriers will be overcome, and the friendship will continue to grow. The point is, friendship is a process.

4. If you have a lifelong best friend, you have an unusual treasure. We have to be realistic about our expectations concerning the number and depth of friendships we'll have.

We have numerous acquaintances — people we meet here and there and with whom we exchange the most superficial facts about ourselves. We may have several pals with whom we do certain activities such as play softball or enjoy talking with when our kids are playing together. Take away the activity, and the relationship tends to fizzle.

We may have quite a few of what Letty Cottin Pogrebin calls confederates. (Think the Lone Ranger and Tonto.) The pair is mutually dependent but rarely equal in power — as seen in business and mentoring relationships. When the weaker party gets strong or the mentoree becomes more effective than the mentor, the bond will break unless a different basis for relating is established. I repeat, we have countless acquaintances; we may have several confederates and pals.

If we're blessed we have a handful of deep friendships. Soul friends can speak a kind of shorthand; between them there's an immediate understanding about what you're thinking and feeling. Time and distance usually doesn't interfere; we stay connected to them in a vital way even if they live across country.

5. Each person has the right to pick her friends. You and I may not be able to choose our family, but even women in ministry may choose their friends. Depending on the size of your church or ministry group, all members will probably be your acquaintances. Some you may choose as pals. Some you'll select as confederates whom you work with or mentor. Your strongest friendship may be in your church or outside your congregation or organization. The point is, nobody has a right to usurp your privilege and responsibility to determine your friendships. By the same token, you don't have a right to decide this for another adult.

6. The level or depth of the relationship must be a mutual decision between two people. Every person has the right to decide how close she's willing to be with another. While all Christians owe others kindness and respect, none of us owes it to another to be best friends — even if a manipulator tells us God told her you were to be her best friend.

7. Healthy friendships are a two-way street. One person doesn't always get to be grumpy, be late, be in crisis, do all the talking, or decide where you'll have lunch. If you're giving more than you're getting, or if you're taking more than you're giving, you can count on experiencing either burnout or guilt in the relationship. Real friendship is about mutuality.

8. The deepest friendships are based on commonality, character, chemistry, and commitment. All friendships require some level of *commonality* — shared interests and ideas. Of course, we tend to choose as friends people whose *character* we affirm. We want to hang out with safe people who are loyal, generous, open, sensitive, accepting, honest, forgiving. We also choose friends based on *chemistry*. As in dating and courtship, chemistry is important in friendships. Some people you just click with, and some you don't — an often undefinable and unexplainable phenomenon. Then there's the element of *commitment;* friends care enough about the relationship to make some promises to each other, whether spoken or unspoken. (Some friends actually make covenants with each other as did David and Jonathan.) The effect is an understanding that each will treat the other well.

9. You can kill a friendship by expecting too much from one person. Nobody on God's earth was designed to be our be-all-and-end-all. Even a best friend tends to get resistant and downright testy if she feels she's expected to fill all our emotional needs. You can suffocate a relationship through unreasonable demands.

10. We often need different friends for different aspects of our personality. For those of us in church leadership, having a number of very good friends, rather than one best friend, may be a wise and practical solution to our need for meaningful relationships. In this scheme of things, we don't deposit all of who we are in one person. With one you laugh. With another you think great thoughts and discuss big ideas. With one you process daily events and happenings — the good and bad events of family and professional life. The benefit of this is limiting the damage in the event of a friend's betrayal.

And just as we have different friends for different aspects of ourselves, we often do well to have friends of different ages.

Especially those of us in ministry benefit by having an older, discreet friend who can serve as a listening ear, wise advisor, and prayer warrior on our behalf.

Don't take this as a recommendation to keep friendships shallow to protect yourself. I'm suggesting that you can go deeply in different areas with different friends of various ages. If, however, God gives what Anne of Green Gables called a bosom friend, gratefully invest in her as one of the Father's greatest gifts.

For Personal Meditation & Group Discussion

Reflect on these verses and write your own principles on friendship. Think of practical ways to apply them.

1. Proverbs 12:26

2. Proverbs 16:28

3. Proverbs 17:9

4. Proverbs 17:17

5. Proverbs 27:6

6. Proverbs 27:9-10

7. Ecclesiastes 4:9-12

Dear Friend,

I went to an overnight retreat for pastors' wives in Minnesota. The site was a lovely Marriott in downtown Minneapolis. Breakfast was served in bed, thanks to room service ordered for all participants. I could get used to that kind of pampering!

We did some fun get-acquainted things such as talking with another person about whether we'd rather break a promise or break a heart, and whether we'd rather lose $100 or pay a $100 driving fine. Fellowship was as rich as the Alfredo sauce on the linguine and the dessert of cheesecake we had for lunch.

I was asked to speak on the subject of friendship. To collect some data on friendships and the women at the retreat, I took a survey. When asked what qualities they looked for in a friend, "trustworthy" and "fun/sense of humor" tied for the highest number of mentions. 1) Transparency and genuineness, 2) keeping confidences, 3) caring and compassionate, and 4) accepting, nonjudgmental, a good listener received the same number of votes to win second place.

All those responding to the survey felt they were a good friend, but two said they'd never had a best friend. The group was equally split about whether or not one could have too many friends. Almost all, however, said they continue to make new friends. Eleven noted they'd had a serious disagreement with a close friend, and yet the friendship survived for nine of them. The women split about whether or not one's husband should be her best friend; half said he should be, but an equal number believed a woman needs a best friend in addition to her husband. Those who believe they could have a best friend in the church often noted that this required skill and work.

The question was asked, "What do you do together?" The answers were varied: play, laugh, talk, do church work, minister, drink coffee, do lunch, celebrate birthdays, visit in person and via phone, encourage, pray, worship, shop, do crafts, get together with the children, go out for dinner, walk, dream, go to a play or movie, participate in Bible study, hold each other accountable.

Some noted long-distance friendships and mentioned how they shopped for great phone rates so they could talk regularly and at some length. (I recommend this. An hour of phone conversation is a heap less expensive than an hour of psychotherapy — and perhaps more sanity preserving.)

I trust you have a soul friend or two.

Warmly,

Pamela

24
Avoiding Mouth Traps

Just because we're physically capable of talking and hearing doesn't mean we communicate well.

People find communication difficult for many reasons. A major one has to do with our family of origin. If we were raised by yellers, naggers, exaggerators, criticizers, demanders, or whiners, we may suffer the lack of good early models. If our parents used silence to punish when they felt upset or offended, we may have picked up the same passive-aggressive way of expressing our hurt or disapproval. Maybe we grew up in an environment where kids were to be seen and not heard, so home didn't provide a safe laboratory for practicing communication skills.

A low opinion of oneself is another factor inhibiting good communication. If we think our thoughts, feelings, dreams, choices, and preferences are silly, unimportant, or worthless, chances are we have a hard time sharing openly and honestly with others. Furthermore, when we undervalue ourselves, we often overvalue what others say, think, and feel — especially in regard to us — and we give their opinions and ideas undue weight.

Some of us don't communicate well simply because we've never thought much about it. Yet the Bible encourages us to give good thought to it in its advice about speaking, listening, controlling the tongue, and the attitudes we express both verbally and nonverbally. In other words, the Scripture-Inspirer says this is an important subject, so let's take a run at it. Let's focus on the mouth even though we acknowledge that listening is at least as important as speaking in communication.

Keep the Goal in Mind

Communication is key to understanding others, being understood, and developing relationships. We mutually disclose information about ourselves on increasingly deeper levels if we want to develop an increasingly closer and more meaningful friendship.

Jill told me that ten years ago her friend asked, "Who would you say is your best friend?" Jill responded, "You are!" Then the friend said, "But I hardly know you. You seem to have this invisible barrier around you. You don't really let me know you." At that point Jill decided to risk being her honest-to-goodness (and even honest-to-badness) self so that the friendship could deepen.

Even when communicating with adversaries, our goal is greater understanding of and love for our opponents. We devalue people when our purpose is to vanquish them in a war of words. We create ill will when our winning requires others' losing, when our viewpoint must prevail to the extent that we'll use whatever verbal and emotional force is necessary to gain victory for our position. We can win an argument and leave the loser's mind unchanged and heart hardened against us and whatever truth we may be proclaiming. On the other hand, when we can communicate respectfully and lovingly with people whose beliefs and values we may not embrace, we keep the door open to further dialogue and friendship.

Lovingly Truthful, Truthfully Loving

The Scripture is clear that we're to speak the truth in love. Make no mistake about it: It's truth *and* love, not truth *or* love.

On the truth side, we've met people who say with pride, "I just tell it like it is!" In reality, they try to excuse rudeness and harshness by claiming a certain superiority in being honest. The result often is leaving a trail of bruises and blood as their tongue pummels people. It's one thing if the truth hurts, it's another to inflict hurt by the way we express truth.

We've also met people who were less than honest in the name of being loving. Their desire to please and not offend often leads them to misrepresent, deny, or outright lie about what they really believe, think, or feel. In the long run, they usually end up hurting both themselves and others anyway.

Ephesians 4:15 links the ability to speak both lovingly and truthfully with spiritual maturity. For most of us this takes practice. How much? For me it's been decades, and I'm still not all grown up in this area. At times I still want to use my mouth to blast people with the truth; at other times I want so much for people to like me (at least not reject me) that I'm less than candid when I know what I think is at odds with their thoughts. I take some consolation in knowing I'm making progress even though I'm not perfect.

Common Mouth Traps

What does speaking the truth in love look like? Perhaps it will help to consider some common ways people's mouths get them into trouble and hinder connection with others.

Exaggerating. Exaggeration is often our attempt to appear bigger, smarter, braver, or more pathetic than we really are. Sometimes there's a place for stretching the truth for the sake of fun — making a humorous point — but the exaggeration should be obvious. The problem is that if we stretch the truth as a way of life, people regularly feel the need to cut what we say in half. They never know if we were really as sick as we claimed or if our kid was truly as successful as we said or if the situation was as dramatic as we expressed it. We undermine trust.

Sometimes we exaggerate to strengthen our argument so we can vanquish the foe. Such truth-stretching statements often begin with "You always…" "You never…" "I always have to…" "I never get to…." Closely related to that kind of all-or-none statement are authoritarian generalities we pull out to strengthen an argument: "Women aren't capable of leadership." "Good mothers don't work outside the home." "No godly person can be a Democrat." We hate it when others pull that junk on us, so we can expect negative reactions when we pull it on others.

Accusing You-Statements. Expressing our thoughts and feelings with you-statements rather than I-statements is another mouth trap which catches too many of us. Negative you-statements condemn; I-statements explain.

Judgmental or accusatory you-statements begin with "You

are..." and end with words like mean, unfair, stupid, ugly, unreasonable, irresponsible, and unspiritual. They attack and demean the person. They may tell more about the speaker than they express the reality of the person she's characterizing.

I-statements help us express what we're thinking and feeling. They let others know what's going on inside us. They allow us to tell the truth about ourselves. "I'm angry." "I'm embarrassed." "I feel hurt when you tease me about my weight." "I believe this." "I think the facts say that." "I wish you had told me that in private."

While we have a right to own what's going on inside our skins and express it, we're not obligated to share everything that pops into our heads. Even before using I-statements, it may help to ask ourselves: Will sharing this mutually benefit the other person and me? Will expressing this truth in love make a better relationship possible?

Speaking for Others. More than once I've run into people who spoke for others to try to strengthen the point they were making. One time a man made a negative you-statement to me. We'd never spent time together either socially or in a work situation, or exchanged more than superficial words of greeting. So I said to him, "I'm not sure how you came to that conclusion since you don't know me very well." He replied, "Others think this way, too." I knew who our mutual friends were and had every reason to believe they didn't share his opinion of me. He spoke for others, and that's fighting dirty rather than communicating truth in love.

We're out of line when we hear ourselves making negative you-statements to another and then saying, "I've talked to some others and they feel the same way." Or, "Most people don't like your idea." Or, "When the group said this to you, they really meant that." Something unhealthy is going on inside us when we dare speak for others. We're presuming we have a right to express their thoughts and feelings (at least we perceive them to think and feel that way) to bolster our position.

Each of us can and should speak only for ourselves. In reality, we only know for sure what's inside our own heads and hearts. We need to have the courage to say, "I feel..." or "I think..." or "I believe...." Period. If we don't want to stand on our own two feet in communication, then we'd do well to keep quiet rather than resort to secondhand testimony.

I'd even like to throw in a caution about speaking for God, which can be arrogant at best and destructive at worst. It's one thing to say, "The Bible (or even God) says..." and then quote a passage of Scripture. It's another thing to assume our interpretation or application of Scripture is infallible. We need some humility here! Even when we believe we're 100 percent correct in our understanding of what's right and wrong, we're still under obligation to express that truth in love.

Ultimatums & Threats. When we were kids we may have said, "If I can't have my way, I'm going to hold my breath till I die." Or, "Play by my rules, or I'll take my ball and go home." Such communication is the hallmark of immaturity.

Threats and ultimatums are a dead giveaway that we're feeling angry and/or desperate. We can go ahead and use them if we will, but we'd better understand how much power we're putting into others' hands. We're allowing them to decide our course of action. More than one clergy family found themselves out of a job when they issued an ultimatum to do it my way or I leave! The moral of the story is clear: Never issue a threat or an ultimatum unless you're happily willing to abide by the choice of another.

Seasoning with Salt

Our speech is to be with grace and seasoned with salt (Col. 4:6). Salt makes food more palatable. It has preserving qualities that prevent spoiling and rotting. Salt-seasoned speech is gracing speech.

Speaking graciously with love makes truth more palatable, easier for others to digest. Speaking graciously with love as well as truth helps preserve relationships and keeps them from spoiling. (By the way, when we find ourselves saying, "I'm telling you this because I love you," we need to ask ourselves whom we're trying to convince. Love is seldom revealed simply by our declarations.)

Speaking truth with grace is the target at which we aim. The more we hit it, the more we are like the One who came "full of grace and truth" (John 1:14).

For Personal Meditation & Group Discussion

1. We can regret words spoken and words left unspoken. Consider experiences you've had in each category. What did you learn from them?

2. James 1:19 exhorts us to be slow to speak, and Proverbs 10:19, 17:28, and 21:23 encourage the same. As you study these passages, what does the Holy Spirit say to you?

3. Sometime read Proverbs and highlight every verse pertaining to speech. For now, reflect on 11:12, 12:6, 12:18-19, 15:2, 15:4, 16:27, 17:4, 17:20, 18:21, 21:6, 22:11, 25:15, 25:23, 26:28, and 28:23. If you put truth on one end of a continuum and love/grace on the other, where do you think you fall on that line?

4. Read James 3:5-10. What does it say? What does it mean? How does it apply to you personally?

5. If you take pride in speaking the truth, consider the balance 1 Corinthians 13:1-3 may bring to your communication.

6. One of the characteristics of the Proverbs 31 woman is that "she speaks with wisdom" (v. 26). In your own words, how would you define speaking with wisdom? What adjectives would you use?

7. If your speech reflects your spiritual vitality and maturity as James 1:26 suggests, where do you stand in your walk of faith?

Dear Friend,

Words can positively destroy a person, mangling her self-image, self-worth, self-esteem, self-efficacy. I've known people who have suffered their entire lives because the negative and abusive messages they heard about themselves long ago still roll around in their heads, haunting them with feelings of inadequacy, ugliness, and defectiveness. Certainly broken bones heal more easily than wounded souls.

For a while now I've lived with the totally false assumption that every adult understands the importance of her words and the basics of good communication. Observation has disabused me of that idea. I can't tell you how many times I've inwardly shuddered when a person told me, "So, I just said to her (or him or them)..." and then I listened with amazement as a truly offensive statement came out of her mouth. I was amazed that she was amazed that what she said got such a negative result!

I became interested in gaining communication skills when this talker found herself married to a man who was the strong, *silent* type. I believed more than three decades ago — and I still do — that communication is a big key to a satisfying marriage. So I began to read books and we attended seminars galore. I learned that by practicing certain elementary rules, we could improve our communication and our relationship.

Since whole books are written about communication, a little chapter like this can't begin to do more than scratch the surface in dealing with the subject. Yet I offer this with the prayer that it will be helpful. More than that, I hope it will whet your appetite to study the subject further. The time you invest will reap great dividends. Practicing good communication skills could improve your marriage, strengthen your connection with your children, increase your understanding and influence, disarm the disgruntled, keep you from regularly immersing yourself in hot water, and express the love of Jesus more fully.

Having said this, I need you to know I haven't arrived as a communicator. I'm still learning, so I need others' patience when I blow it in personal communication. I intend to be patient with others as well. I also commit not to act the role of "talk police and judge," so people don't feel the need to clam up on me!

Warmly,

Pamela

25

Is It a Backpack or Burden?

Do you ever feel as if a cast of hundreds is asking for a piece of you, and there's not enough of you to go around? Your husband wants this, your kids need that, church members have their expectations, and your mom is making demands.

It's not as if you don't love people. As a Christian you want to serve them. You take seriously your responsibility to show practical love by ministering to others' needs.

The problem is that we Christians sometimes have a hard time determining what needs we can and should help meet and what needs people must tend to themselves. We get confused about how to act responsibly toward another without taking responsibility for him or her. And when our caregiving crosses the line into caretaking, we often get exhausted, angry, and can even burn out.

In our society women are socialized to be helpers, nurturers, and caregivers in such a way that it's easy to think that we must rescue, fix, and take care of people's feelings, opinions, needs, wishes, expectations, and problems regardless of the personal cost to ourselves. If the tendency to take care of people is doubled for us because we're women, it's doubled again for those of us in the people-helping professions. In short, many of us have a problem with boundaries.

Defining Boundaries

What are boundaries? Boundaries are invisible fences, if you will, that mark off what's ours from what's not ours. They differentiate you from me and me from you. They define who and what we are and what we must take responsibility for.

Think of your skin as the boundary that surrounds your property. What's contained within your skin is what you're responsible for — your feelings, thoughts, wants and wishes, choices, behaviors, gifts and talents, beliefs, likes and dislikes, attitudes, values, and your standard of what behaviors you'll accept or tolerate from others and what you won't. Because each person is one of a kind, what's contained within our skin boundary is unique. That's why boundaries define us.

Because all that's within my skin belongs to me, nobody else is responsible for my feelings, thoughts, wants and wishes, choices, behaviors, gifts and talents, beliefs, attitudes, likes and dislikes, values, and my standard of what behaviors I'll accept or tolerate from others and what I won't. This is all mine to own and deal with.

At the same time, I'm not responsible for your feelings, thoughts, wants and wishes, choices, behaviors, gifts and talents, beliefs, attitudes, likes and dislikes, values, priorities and your standards of what behaviors you'll accept or tolerate from others and what you won't. That's all yours to own and deal with.

Backpacks and Burdens

Galatians 6:2 and 5 talks about this issue in terms of burdens and loads: "Carry each other's burdens, and in this way you will fulfill the law of Christ... for each one should carry his [her] own load."

These verses sound contradictory, but they're not. The word "burden" (v. 2) carries with it the idea of excess weight, a crushing mass, a backbreaking or spirit-breaking pressure. Burdens are too much for a person to bear alone; she or he needs help. They are the unusual stresses, crises, traumas, catastrophes, and disasters of life.

The word "load" (v. 5) means the daily workload or toil we each must deal with. It's the inevitable and inescapable cargo we lug around just because we're human. This is the stuff within our boundaries. I call it our backpack. Paul says this is the stuff that each person must carry for herself or himself.

Sometimes we or others treat burdens like a backpack so that we refuse to ask for help we truly need. This is unhealthy independence that may make us unnecessarily stressed and sick.

Sometimes we and others treat backpacks as burdens. This is where ministry wives often get trapped. Others — husband, children, parents, friends, church members — expect us to take responsibility to carry the daily load that's theirs to shoulder, the issues only they themselves can resolve.

A Personal Example

I need wisdom to distinguish between burdens and backpacks. I can drive myself crazy trying to carry loads that don't belong to me. On the other hand, I lack love and I sin when I refuse to help carry others' burdens. Sometimes I've been good at drawing these boundaries and holding firm when people try to violate them, and sometimes I've not been good at this.

When I had a limited psychotherapy practice, I would hear clients' sad, frustrating, and tragic stories. I cared deeply about these people and wanted so badly for them to find wholeness and holiness, but I didn't get burdened down by the horrible problems my clients had. When I was with them, I would show empathy and share my insights. Once I left them, however, I didn't haul them like a weight around my neck. I knew I wasn't their rescuer, fixer, healer, or savior. There's only one Savior and the Savior isn't Pamela Heim. I'm very clear on that.

On the other hand, I've had a harder time not carrying my husband's backpack. I've tended to take responsibility for his feelings, which are most definitely inside his skin. He's inclined toward depression, and for years I worked hard when he was down to pull him up; but I finally realized that his feelings are his to deal with, not mine. It's never really helped him or me to act otherwise; in fact, treating his feelings as if they were mine to fix only postponed and confused his process of healing.

If I don't carefully and prayerfully distinguish between backpacks and burdens, then I don't love people very well. I either treat them like immature, incompetent, irresponsible people who can't survive without me (not showing them proper respect), or I build walls against them to protect myself from getting involved and overwhelmed by their problems (not showing them unselfish love).

Played Out in the Parsonage

More than one pastor's wife has told me something like

this, "I'm so tired. There's a woman in my church who's in a bad marriage, her teenager is rebellious, her mother is schizophrenic and her father is alcoholic. She's draining my time and emotional energy." Or I hear, "I try to be there for my husband to encourage and help him. He pours out his problems to me, and I feel weighted down by them. To whom can I pour out my problems?"

In reality, both these scenarios are backpack issues. As much as we'd like to, we can't save another woman from such a family, and we can't fix a husband's problems with his job or even give him self-esteem to empower him in fixing them himself. These are not burdens that God intends for us to carry.

We can take our husband's and many other people's problems and stuff them into our backpack and then feel so weighted down we can hardly function. Then we foolishly think the solution is to find somebody else on whom we can dump the junk we're carrying around. And we get angry when nobody volunteers for that job.

Dealing with Others' Stuff

But how do you and I show concern for others' problems without carrying the stuff that belongs in their backpacks? When a person unloads the sad, bad, painful stuff from his/her backpack onto your kitchen or coffee table (depending on where you're sitting)....

- Listen to everything he/she says.
- Accept that his/her feelings are legitimate and important. Never disallow or disparage a person's feeling, ever.
- Acknowledge the toughness of the situation.
- Empathize with him/her. We weep with those who weep.
- Express confidence in God's ability to give the person

strength and wisdom to make good choices about and solve his or her (it's truly not your) problem. Give hope.
- As God leads, you may pray with the person, share an insight, or recommend a course of action.

If you discover the person really has a burden, you do what you in your limited way can do to help. But if you're dealing with backpack material, when the conversation is over, you mentally pick up all the stuff they've piled onto the table, and you gently stuff it back into their backpack with a silent prayer for them. You do *not* pick it up and cram it in yours. God has made their back strong enough to carry the load they have, but He didn't make your back strong enough to carry the problems and pain of all the people in your world.

Ultimately, others must make choices about how to carry their own loads, and they bear the consequences of those choices. If you don't like their choices, the best you can do is take responsibility for how you choose to handle your feelings and thoughts as it relates to their choices.

A spiritually and emotionally healthy woman knows the difference between backpacks and burdens. She knows what she can and can't do. She always, always, always reminds herself that she's not the fixer, the rescuer, the savior; but she knows Who is and trusts those she loves to Him. Only He, not she, can make others both happy and holy.

For Personal Meditation & Group Discussion

1. In each of the situations below, are you dealing with a backpack or burden? (Some have elements of both.) Determine what you might reasonably do to help and what you can't do.
   - Problem #1: Your adult son is rather irresponsible, needs employment, has bills to pay, but doesn't seem too serious about getting a job.
   - Problem #2: Your mother feels stress (and calls you three times a week about it) because your father's had bypass surgery and he's not following doctor's orders.
   - Problem #3: Your husband is having a major conflict with the chairperson of the church council. He's irritable with you and the children and doesn't sleep well at night.
   - Problem #4: A divorced mom with two little children doesn't get child support, and she has no job skills or experience.
   - Problem #5: Church members seem to think you should take charge of children's church. You have no gifts, skills, or even desire for this ministry.

2. Revisit the story of the Good Samaritan (Luke 10:30-35). What does the Bible say the Good Samaritan did for the man left wounded by the side of the road? Using your imagination, what might he have done but didn't do? (One example: He didn't stick around to make sure the man finally got to Jericho OK.)

3. Read Matthew 19:16-22 and notice how Jesus respected the man's decision. What did Jesus do or not do in response? How do you feel when people try to manipulate or coerce you about choices you make?

4. Consider Judas' betrayal and Peter's denial of Jesus (Mark 14, Matt. 26). To what extent, if any, are you to blame if those closest to you walk away from God?

Dear Friend,

As a young person I sang a song with lyrics that went something like this: "Let me burn and wear out for Thee. Don't let me rust or my life be a failure." The implication is that there are two ways to live — burning out or rusting out, the former being a virtue and the latter being a sin.

Personally, the thought of burnout is about as appealing to me as rust-out. I don't think I score points with God for engaging in a slow form of suicide in the name of ministry. And living according to other people's feelings, thoughts, wants and wishes, choices, behaviors, beliefs, likes and dislikes, attitudes, and values can slowly destroy a person as surely as can inhaling nicotine.

Many women I counsel are wearing themselves out trying to do for others what those others must do for themselves. In the name of being loving, women "mother" their husbands, mortgage their children's future by taking responsibility for things kids need to own themselves, and enable friends and church members to escape the consequences (one of God's best teaching tools) of poor or sinful choices.

I'm impressed that Jesus accomplished so much, but He didn't go through Galilee and Judea like a Jewish tornado. I get the sense that He paced Himself. At least twice He was so busy He didn't stop to eat, but He took time later to regroup His depleted energy. He slept. He got away from the crowds — at times right in the middle of successful evangelistic and healing campaigns. He always took time to be with His Father.

I want to follow Jesus' example. I want to rest in the Father, taking time to let Him restore my soul. I want to listen to the Father's will and do that. I don't want to burn out because I've made others gods before Him — doing their will rather than His — or because I act as if I'm God and must bear the weight of the world on my puny shoulders. Is this your desire also? For your sake and the kingdom's sake, I pray it is.

Warmly,

Pamela

26
Help That Doesn't Harm People

"Do no harm" is a physician's first priority. Helping the patient heal comes on the heels of that. Likewise, as we minister in Jesus' name, not harming people who ask for help is at the top of our list.

In discussing the difference between backpacks and burdens, we considered how to help others without harming ourselves. In this chapter, we look at how to help others without harming them.

Typical Needs for Healing

In the world people do have tribulations (John 16:33). Earth feels the impact of an enemy whose goal is to kill love, destroy peace, and steal hope (John 10:10). He creates chaos among nations, between persons, and within individuals. For those reasons, all of us probably have been called on to minister to somebody whose loved one died, daughter is pregnant out of wedlock, self-esteem is crushed, marriage is a disappointment or disaster, job was terminated, emotional stability crumbled, family member abuses drugs or alcohol, body is malfunctioning or diseased, income doesn't cover expenses, family of origin was unhealthy or abusive, family member is physically or mentally impaired, or faith is faltering under severe testing. (Whew! Doesn't that listing exhaust you?)

Such problems can leave us feeling overwhelmed. We can easily feel powerless because we can't rescue, fix, heal, or save such hurting people. As noted before, there's only one Savior and His name is Jesus. We can, however, offer significant help.

"Help" That Harms: Fixing Myself

Our laudable desire to help others can be wrongly motivated. We can attempt to help a person in order to meet our own needs. When we want to make another feel better so we feel better, that's self-centeredness, not other-centeredness.

Helping usually does more harm than good when motivated by our unresolved, often unconscious, personal needs to control people, to make situations tidy and comfortable, to gain a sense of personal significance and worth, or to earn God's favor.

The flip side of this is that we may stand aloof from needy people if we're pretty sure we can't rescue them. To fail to fix another would miserably aggravate our inadequacies and fears.

"Help" That Harms: Advice

Sometimes we harm people because we assume the role of advisor rather than helper. Advice is a poor substitute for a listening ear, a shoulder to cry on, or prayer.

As a young wife, I had to learn that when my husband

complained about a problem at work he was not asking me to solve it. In fact, by positing solutions I implied that I was smarter than he at figuring out how to fix things. (More than a tad arrogant!) I helped him best by letting him vent, listening with empathy, and expressing my confidence in his ability to deal with the situation. Giving advice is generally not good counseling.

Do we ever give advice? Maybe after we've proved we understand the problem. Perhaps after a long period of time of simply being there for the person. Probably only if we've been *asked* our opinion and we determined that it's genuinely wanted.

Even then we do better to think in terms of sharing our observations and insights: "Here's how it seems to me. How does that square with your perceptions?" Or we explore possible options with the person, being sure to involve her in suggesting potential solutions.

"Help" That Harms: Judging

When people tell us their problems, we sometimes rush to judgment: *She must have messed up her kid badly. She should just forgive and get on with her life. She doesn't sound submissive enough to her husband. She should trust Christ more. She must be disobeying the Word.*

Such thinking often stems from the childish idea that bad stuff only happens to bad people. Those accepting this insupportable premise conclude that the way to solve a person's problems is to listen long enough to pinpoint her sin, explain what the Bible says about it, and tell her to get right with God.

Many hurt people already feel broken, inadequate, imperfect, and sinful. They already don't feel good enough or smart enough or strong enough, so our judgment only compounds their problem.

Even when a person's stresses and wounds are the result of her sin, we still do well to *listen long, empathize accurately, and care genuinely*. Only after we've done that well will any truth we share be helpful.

Help That Helps

How then do we help others? In brief, we help when we give our presence, listening, acceptance, and hope.

Presence. A comforting aspect of our faith is that our God is Immanuel — with us and even in us. He is the Friend who sticks closer than a brother. Unlike human family and friends, He *never* leaves or forsakes us.

Never underestimate the healing of being with a hurting person. Once I went through a tough situation, and my friend Susan came by just to sit with me. She didn't say much, but her presence spoke volumes about her willingness to walk with me through my pain. She incarnated Jesus' presence in a tangible way.

When all is said and done, being there for a person is often more important than what's said and done. That's especially true when we hang in there over the long haul.

Listening. More important than knowing what to say to a needy person is giving her the opportunity to talk and talk and talk — and then talk some more. Listening is at the heart of helping.

Some barriers to listening are: 1) the tendency to want to do the talking — especially too quickly telling our story of similar pain or stress, 2) the compulsion to give advice, 3) getting impatient when we hear the story more than once, 4) being uncomfortable with silence, and 5) hearing only words.

Good listening uses our eyes, head, and heart, as well as ears. What is this person communicating nonverbally? (Tears may be running down her cheeks, but she's smiling and saying she's all right!) What does she seem to be feeling? (Her tone of voice and choice of words can give you clues.) What beliefs are behind her words? (She may think her abuse is her fault.)

I've found that if I truly listen, I sometimes know a person is *not* fine when she answers, "Fine, thank you" to my "How are you?" Sometimes I've responded, "That sounds tentative. Are you really OK?" Sometimes that's opened the door to help her bear a burden.

Good listening verifies what is heard. What you think you hear may not be what the other person thought she said. So check out what you understood her to say: "I hear you saying that you feel ripped you off. Is that accurate?" "Are you saying your son embarrassed you in front of your friends?" "It sounds to me as if you're having a hard time feeling that God cares about you." The important point is assuring the person that she's been heard because you've accurately reflected — paraphrased — her words.

Accepting. We help people when we accept them where they are without judging and condemning them. This is the essence of loving the sinner though hating her sin.

Self-confessed sinners felt comfortable with Jesus because He was gentle and gracious with them. Thieves, prostitutes, and riffraff liked to be with Him, and being with Him changed their lives. Only the self-righteous felt His wrath.

We're more likely to be helpful if people feel safe with and loved by us. We show acceptance when we honor their thoughts and respect their feelings — *never* telling them how they should or shouldn't think and feel. Our acceptance gives people the freedom, courage, and strength to change and heal.

Hope. People needing help often feel helpless and hopeless. We don't tell them a good Christian should be hopeful, but we convey that we have great hope that God will provide a way to handle their problem. Our help will never harm another if we keep our own hope alive for her and express that until she can hope again.

Above all, don't be paralyzed by this caution about not harming those you wish to help. The greatest harm of all is doing nothing because you fear you can't do something perfectly.

For Personal Meditation & Group Discussion

1. Read 2 Samuel 16:23, just one passage that speaks of Ahithophel's advice. What made him a good adviser? Proverbs 27:6 and 9 reveals another qualification for advisers. Note the anger and sarcasm of Job's response to advisers who ignored the two principles just noted (26:1-4).

2. What do Proverbs 17:17, 18:24 and Ecclesiastes 4:9-12 say about hanging in there with hurting, needy people? Now study Psalm 55:12-14 to appreciate the pain we can inflict when we let friends down.

3. Remind yourself of the harm of judging by reading Matthew 7:1-2, Romans 14:3-4, and James 4:12. Note Jesus' example in Luke 12:14, John 3:16-18, 8:11, 8:15-16, 12:47-48 and Romans 8:1.

4. Not judging is the negative side of the positive aspect of accepting and forgiving as encouraged in Romans 15:7, Ephesians 4:32 and 1 Peter 3:8. Meditate on these passages.

5. How do Philippians 2:3-4, Romans 12:10, 1 Corinthians 10:24, and 1 Peter 4:10 speak to meeting one's own needs in the guise of helping others?

6. What principles for harmless helping do you gain from Ephesians 4:29 and James 1:19?

Dear Friend,

I've received so much help over the years of my life, and I've suffered some real crises.

I know doctrine and Scripture and ideas about why a good God allows bad things to happen. I know God's promises and have clutched them for dear life. Still, I've needed friends to minister to me.

Thank God, I have a family and a couple of very good friends. I have a wonderful family in Christ across our country. I've been deeply touched and encouraged by the notes and letters I've received from the latter to let me know of their prayers and love:

- Judy in California reminded me that God is holding on to me even if grief robs me of the ability to hang on to Him.
- Marie in Minnesota mentioned how good God has been to her but gave me permission to feel that He wasn't being very good to me in my present circumstance.
- Rosemary in Iowa told me my situation sounded like a Peretti novel and then told me how she and others were standing with me in the spiritual battle I've been going through.

In short, my dear sisters in Christ heard my hurt and wept with me. They didn't harm me by offering advice or suggesting easy solutions. They didn't criticize me, but accepted me where and as I was. They gave me the security of knowing I was being fervently prayed for on those days I could not pray for myself. (Have you discovered how much energy it takes to pray!?)

I hope you're that kind of friend to others. I pray that you have friends like that.

Warmly,

Pamela

27

Is the Woman Driving You Crazy?

She's terrific. She's dedicated, so faithful in church attendance. She serves on committees and accepts responsibility. You can count on her to volunteer when you need help. She's gifted in organizing and leading. She's a good Bible study teacher or worship leader.

She's your friend; you enjoy spending time with her. She makes you feel safe enough to share some things you don't normally talk about with others in your congregation. She's generous, sometimes surprising you with gifts.

Women in your church *love* her and emulate her as an example of a godly woman. They cluster around her, vying for her time and the privilege of being in her inner circle.

A Fly in the Ointment

So it dismays you when stuff she says and does begins to

annoy you, and the pile of her offenses increases. You tell yourself nobody's perfect and try to overlook her troublesome behaviors.

For one thing, she's possessive of you and your time. When you hit garage sales one Saturday morning with another friend, she lets you know on Sunday that she's hurt you didn't invite her. She wants to be treated like your best and only friend even if she's not. Indeed, she seems to need to be the center of attention for many church women.

She works on projects, maybe even in the church office, so that she's in proximity to your husband. She consults him, helps him, advises him. One pastor's wife described her as "the other woman." She wasn't talking about illicit sex, but about the woman's apparent bent to usurp the place of the pastor's wife in the church's (and even the pastor's) life.

It's Your Imagination

You decide to concentrate on her good qualities — how gifted she is, how much she does in the church — but it grows increasingly hard for you to ignore the negative aspects of her personality. You tell yourself you're being petty, critical, and maybe jealous. You suspect that you're the one with a problem. After all, nobody else seems to have a problem with her.

You pray a lot about your attitude. You confess to God sins real and imaginary. You try harder with her, go out of your way to be nice. Nothing seems to work, however, because she really does annoy the stew out of you.

You decide to be more honest with her and challenge her lovingly when you feel she's out of line. When you do, you see a side of her you've not seen before. She acts like you've just escaped from a locked hospital ward. She doesn't apologize. She defends herself mightily and then goes on the offensive. How could you be so unChristian as to judge her? After all she's done for you, how can you be so ungrateful? She shoots Bible verses at you like they're bullets. She manages to convince you what you feared all along — the real problem is you.

You buy this for a while, but one day you learn some others share your concerns. Perhaps your husband or an elder spoke to the woman about issues of concern, and she started talking around the church about how unspiritual the leaders are. It seems that anybody who doesn't recognize how wonderful she is needs to get right with God! An article in *Leadership Journal* called women like this "Bright, Beautiful, and Deeply Disturbed."

Up Close and Personal

Kathy talked to me about such a woman.* The woman was gifted. She helped lead worship and worked in the church office. Kathy's and the woman's families connected socially with some frequency — a natural outcome of spending so much time together in ministry.

Women clustered around her. They raved about her Bible class. Slowly but surely she did a good job of pushing Kathy to the margins of church life. She steadily displaced Kathy as leader in one ministry and another. One particularly obnoxious habit was the way she regularly pounced on Kathy when she was talking to somebody else at church and thrust herself into the conversation. When Kathy confronted her about her problematic behaviors, Kathy ended up feeling to blame.

The woman put in lots of gifted effort that helped the church grow; but when it did, she seemed to resent turning over some of her leadership responsibilities to newly hired staff.

After the pastor and an elder challenged her about her attitude, she started criticizing the church's leaders to any member who would give her a hearing. Attempts to talk to her about this only ended with her call for the leaders to repent of their gross — to her — sins against her innocent self.

Common Characteristics of Wounded People

When counseling about this kind of situation, I often ask, "Do you know anything about her family of origin? Did she come from an alcoholic home? An abusive home?" (It sounds like such a shrinky thing to ask, but what would you expect from a psychotherapist?!) That's because hurt people tend to hurt people and create chaos. They've often developed harmful patterns of behaving and relating to others that are deeply ingrained in their personalities.

Understanding this doesn't excuse troubling behavior by troubled persons, but it can help explain it. Though such insight doesn't change the situation, it allows for realistic expectations about what you can and can't do to correct it. Here are some common characteristics often expressed by wounded and wounding people:

1. They may see things in extremes — black and white, good and bad. Consequently, they may start off idolizing a person (*you!*), see normal human flaws, and then react harshly. ("I thought you were loving, but you're like all the rest.")

2. They may have a strong need to control. To control, they may work to get close to you, your husband (sometimes through you), or whomever they consider the center of power in the church. Since knowledge is power, being close to decision-makers means they won't be surprised by new information; in fact, they may even help shape decisions. They love the

power of confidential information, but may use it hurtfully to gain a personal advantage. They can use power in passive-aggressive ways, so subtle others may not readily identify their control motivation.

3. They commonly see disagreements as win-lose situations (and they have to win) because they can't conceive of such a thing as a win-win outcome. Apologizing is often difficult because it's an admission not that they've done wrong, but that they're bad. (See #1 again.)

4. They may seek up-front ministries because of their low self-esteem. Being praised for their teaching, singing, or leading lets them know they have value. Remove them from a highly visible ministry, and you'll hear their screams of agony. Because of their obvious spiritual gifts, knowledge of the Bible, and dedicated service, their self-centeredness may astound you. Sometimes it seems that they give in order to get — serving others to meet their own needs.

5. They may thrive on chaos. They grew up with it. It's familiar to them. Life feels abnormal when things are peaceful. As a result, they may create turmoil. They sometimes have a history of troubling one church and then another.

6. Because of an emotional deficit, a hole in their soul, they never feel they get enough affirmation and love. They can exhaust you and five other people with their subtle and not-so-subtle expectations and demands for attention, help, and recognition. They tend to demand constant proof that you care.

7. They're usually oblivious to their problems. They unconsciously developed mechanisms to cope with life, and they may not have a clue that those unhealthy coping mechanisms are harmful to themselves and others. Thus, they're genuinely baffled — and furious — when anybody points out problems

they're creating.

What Can You Do?

Here are some practical steps you can take to take care of yourself as you deal with the difficult person in your life.

1. Tell yourself three times a day, "I'm not crazy." Trust your observations and your godly insights about the troubled and troubling person, especially if others you respect as wise and good have confirmed them.

2. Realize that you can't help her unless she wants to be helped, and that starts with her being open to feedback and acknowledging her issues (central to confessing her sins).

3. Treat her with cordial respect as you do all church members, but don't feel obligated to love her as a best friend. You have a right to choose who will be close to you.

4. Set boundaries with her — this is a good example. Do God's will and be true to the way He's made you and refuse to let her control how you'll think, feel, act, choose, and spend your time. She may be a victim, but you don't have to be her victim.

5. Don't talk to her alone if past conversations have resolved nothing and left you in shreds. It may sound paranoid, but remember that to her communication is not about exchanging information but about conquering. To win she may painfully distort your words to your face or destructively spread untrue gossip later. In extreme cases, her need to win has resulted in lawsuits.

6. Understand that probably she's a problem to the church as well as you. Let church leaders — pastors and elders — handle her if she's affecting the health of the body. You as a pastor's wife are a Christian leader, but you probably don't have the

official leadership role that is responsible for church discipline.

7. Pray for her. Pray for yourself. You need God's wisdom, courage, and compassion to deal with her.

8. Give yourself permission to grieve her loss if she betrayed the friendship you gave her.

9. Forgive her. Remember, however, forgiveness is not the same as reconciliation. A restored relationship may only be possible if she repents.

Both Kathy and the woman are a composite of several pastors' wives and several difficult women.

For Personal Meditation & Group Discussion

1. How do you feel about the fact that Jesus took Peter, James, and John into His inner circle and didn't include the other nine apostles in that intimate group? Do you allow yourself that kind of freedom in relating to women in your church?

2. Look at what Revelation 12:10 calls Satan. What kind of accusations does he make through the difficult woman in your life? Which of them bothers you most? What did Jesus call Satan? (See John 8:44 for a clue.) What's the truth about you as you deal with crazy-making people?

3. What kind of things might you pray for God to do for your troubling woman? (Other than remove her to another church!) What kind of things do you pray for yourself as you seek to be blameless in your relationship with her? Write these lists down and pray these requests every day until God grants you release.

4. Read Dan Allender's book, *Bold Love,* for insight on what forgiving means in dealing with different kinds of difficult people.

Dear Friend,

All of us ministry women at some time or other run across that person who bugs the daylights out of us. Some of them just never seemed to learn good manners and social skills. They're annoying, but it's usually easy to cut them some slack. Some have unpleasant personalities, and most people find them hard to be around.

But the person I'm talking about in this chapter is charming, intelligent, gifted, and very troubled. One psychologist calls such a person "crazy-making." Surely it can make you feel crazy when she's done such a great job of masking her problematic thinking and behavior that she appears wonderful to most others, and your perception is that she's out of kilter.

Though you feel sane around others, such people make you feel like you're missing something or losing it. The relational skills you practice with others just don't seem to work with them. In fact, sometimes when you try to communicate (wrongfully thinking that any problem can be solved with good communication), it's like you're speaking English to a person who only understands Majang.* You keep thinking that, if you hang in there long enough and show them enough love, surely you can resolve your problems with them. You devote an incredible amount of time, energy, emotion, and prayer to them; but you wish you were directing some of that attention more fruitfully.

I hope this chapter gives you perspective about dealing with such troubling and troubled people and helps you be at peace if you're experiencing such a problem now. If you're not, you probably know somebody who is relating to a crazy-making person. Maybe this will help you walk with her through the situation.

Warmly,

Pamela

*Majang is a language of some people in Ethiopia.

A Concluding Note

28

The View from Retirement

When I learned that the husband of my friend Mariette Seiffert had retired, I took the opportunity to sit down with her for a conversation. I believe you'll appreciate the insights this veteran woman in ministry shared with me.

Mariette, where and when did your ministry with Larry begin?

Our first church was in Glenwood, Minnesota. We moved there on May 28, 1957, and our first child was born that same day!

Whew! Two major adjustments at once. I'm impressed that you lived to tell about it. I know you have more than one child. More important to me, you have grandchildren.

We have four daughters and 12 grandchildren ranging in

age from 4 to 15.

We sometimes hear ministry couples talk about the negative affects of ministry life on their children. Can you tell of some positive benefits your children have realized because their dad was a pastor?

As I look at our daughters' lives and watch them in their own homes, I can't help but be excited at the way they relate to hurting people and also at the high value they put on the church.

That is encouraging. As you look back over almost 40 years in ministry, other than raising a caring family, what has been a highlight?

I was a pastor's wife for 27 years in a local church before Larry became a denominational executive. In each of the local churches we served, I was involved in women's lives. The greatest thing was to see ladies realize that God loves them. His love gave them the energy not to give up on themselves or their marriages.

Highlights suggests there are times of "lowlights." What have been the difficult parts of ministry for you and what got you through them?

It's been very hard to leave people whom I've learned to love and appreciate and then start all over forming new friendships in a new area. I've made an effort, however, to keep old friendships alive by phone and letter. Today I feel rich because of my long-distance and long-time friendships.

I know you and Larry believe ministry couples need to get off the pedestal and be honest about who they are and what they're dealing with. You and I know pastors' wives who

experience grief, depression, or deep woundedness. Some think they have to paste on a smile at church, even when they're dying inside. What would you say to women who feel that way?

Let me answer that question with a question: How can others see God is the answer to our problems if we never reveal that we need Him? One of the things I realize is that some of my best friends today are people I allowed to help me.

We've both heard that God often answers our prayers for help through other people. What I hear you say is that, unless we're willing to be real with others about our needs, we may be cutting ourselves off from one of God's primary ways of ministering to us.

Yes! Pastors' wives need to keep in mind that they, and not just people in the congregation, need the church and the support it can give. I'd like to say to every pastor's wife, "Don't even think of going it alone!" I've personally found God has supplied people to walk with me through hard times if they've known my need. There has always been someone a few steps ahead of me modeling the way.

What I hear in that statement, Mariette, is an admission that "the first lady of the church" doesn't have to be a few steps ahead of every other church woman. I think that many ministry wives, even those who are young, put themselves under tremendous pressure by assuming they're to be the models of maturity in all aspects of life. You're saying members of your congregations have served as examples to you and could help you because in some areas they were farther along in the journey than you. So members can be our friends in time of need. Don't I remember your once saying

The View from Retirement / 305

that we in leadership must remember that the members of our church are not the enemy? Will you please expand on that?

Church people are a gift from God to us. Our responsibility is to appreciate and value the people God supplies to us and our church. We must work together if ministry is to be effective and even enjoyable. I think ministry couples sometimes forget that they're on the same team with church members. Remembering that we and the church are one team requires us to let them see how they are a part of any successes. If we do that, it will be only natural that they will find it easier to share in the difficulties and burdens also.

I like that. The ministry couple isn't one team opposing the church team. In an effective church, pastor and people unite to build the kingdom of God. Yet I'm sure neither of us believes that harmony in the body of Christ comes easily — maybe not even naturally. After all, we in ministry are dealing with wounded and sinful people — but then church members have to relate to wounded and sinful leaders as well. So, can you give a word to pastors' wives about what is rock-bottom essential to their ministry in a less-than-perfect church and world?

Rock bottom? Don't neglect your relationship with God. Above all, keep your love for God alive and growing.

For Personal Meditation & Group Discussion

1. Read 1 John and highlight every reference made to love. Try to distill into one paragraph John's teaching on love. How can you apply this in your relationship with your church? What makes loving difficult for you?

2. Study 1 Corinthians 12. Think of various people in your church and see if you can name the part of the body they are. What part of the body do you think you are? How is God using all of you *together* to do His work in your community?

3. Now consider 1 Corinthians 13. Fruitful ministry is done by Spirit-gifted, Spirit-powered people, but note the spiritual quality foundational to all else. Why do you think that is basic? Do you think people in your church know you love them? Why or why not?

4. Note the command in James 5:16. What keeps ministry wives from obeying this command? Does obeying this command require you to tell your every fault to everybody? What are some guidelines about what to share with whom? How does obeying this command express love for God and others? Note the benefit of obedience to this command. Do you think this benefit is solely in the physical realm?

5. At the end of your life, would it be enough for you if people could say, "She loved God and people"? Why or why not?

The View from Retirement / 307

Dear Friend,

Is time our friend or our enemy? We may perceive it as an enemy because of our youth-glorifying culture. Or when we wonder what's happened to our energy and why we don't have the stamina we once had. Or when we feel the negative physical and emotional problems that can accompany menopause. You understand that I speak from experience here!

But as one who just celebrated her 39th birthday for about the 19th time, I also know time is a friend. It is key to experience-gained wisdom. If we're open to learning, God's Spirit has a way of using life to teach us. Everybody grows old, but those who truly mature do so because of grace and truth applied over *time*.

Time puts things in perspective. A saintly older woman once said to me, "The problem with life is that it's so *daily*." Indeed, in the middle of our dailiness most of us find it easy to lose perspective. Every now and then I find myself fretting over clutter, another's angry words or thoughtless acts, a dashed hope, a thwarted plan, a dumb mistake. Before I invest too much of myself in whining and sniveling, I try to remember to ask, "Does this matter even a smidgen in the light of eternity?" Often, I can't imagine that in the ages to come I'll even remember the hassle that's absorbing my attention so exhaustively at the minute.

Mariette Seiffert speaks as a person to whom time has brought wisdom and perspective. She's one of those mature women referred to in Titus 2. Any of us younger than she (even if only just a little younger!) do well to hear what she has to say.

There's a profoundness in the simplicity of her insight that we ministry wives are called basically to only two things: loving God and loving others. We spend all of our lives learning how to do those two things better.

Loving God and people isn't always easy, however. Sometimes we'll echo Saint Theresa, who wrote that it's no wonder God doesn't have more friends, seeing how He treats those He does have. And occasionally we're in touch with the thinking of the "Peanuts" character who said, "I love mankind. It's people I can't stand."

When we find this business of loving difficult, it often helps to share that problem with a friend. I trust that you're connected to friends, especially friends who are also ministry wives, and that those relationships help you keep perspective over the long haul of ministry.

Warmly,

Pamela